BATTERY LIFE

CLARILUZ GRAHAM

© 2020 Divine Works Publishing LLC.
BATTERY LIFE

ALL RIGHTS RESERVED. No part of this publication may be reproduced, stored in a retrieval system, or transmitted in any form or by any means, electronic, mechanical, photocopying, recording or otherwise without the prior permission of the publisher or in accordance with the provisions of the Copyright, Designs, and Patents Act 1988 or under the terms of any license permitting limited copying issued by the Copyright Licensing Agency.

The views expressed in this work are solely those of the author and do not necessarily reflect the views of the publisher, the publisher hereby disclaims any responsibility for them.

Printed in the United States of America
First Edition: 2021

Scripture taken from the King James Version®., (unless otherwise noted), Copyright © 1982 by Thomas Nelson. Used by permission. All rights reserved.

ISBN 13: 978-1-949105-25-4 (Hardback)
ISBN 13: 978-1-949105-26-1 (eBook)

Published by:
Divine Works Publishing, LLC
Royal Palm Beach, Florida USA

www.DivineWorksPublishing.com
561-990-BOOK (2665)

Dedication

*This book is dedicated to my amazing husband,
Nicholas Graham, you have seen in me what I could not see
in myself. You have challenged me at every juncture of my
journey. You have pushed me past my comfort zone
and for that I thank you.*

*To my children Roman and Charlotte, I write this book so that
you know that the journey you pick is not mine, but yours.
I will always support the dreams and visions that God has
placed in you. I could not have asked for a better gift in the
both of you because you are the best pieces of me who propel me
to grow in all the areas of my life.*

*To my tia Yazmin, thank you for your love and friendship.
You will remain in my hear forever.*

*To my hero, my father Manuel Del Villar,
thank you for your love and your militant values.
You rest in my heart forever.*

Table of Contents

A WELL-POWERED BATTERY *1*

BATTERY COMPOSITION *7*

SELECTING A RECHARGING STATION *19*

CORROSION *33*

REDOX REACTIONS *45*

CURRENT DISRUPTOR *63*

EROSION *73*

INHIBITORS *83*

FEAR *91*

BATTERY BALANCING *95*

BATTERY POSITION *101*

IMAGINATIVE POWER *109*

Acknowledgments

I am thankful to my heavenly father for providing me every tool I needed to develop this book. I am grateful to the set apart spirit of Elohim who assisted me through every letter, word, and sentence in this book.

Nicholas Graham over the years, you constantly reminded me of the urgency of operating with all cylinders firing in my faith. You have been a great teacher and guide for me. I could not have written this book without your on-time words. Thank you for being an awesome father and taking over while I was developing this book. You are the best team player the G squad could have asked for; you are truly the most valuable player! You are the epitome of optimism. My battery power is stronger with you because we share the same power source.

To my bonus parents, Ruben and Aleyda Cordoba an extension of marriage does not even begin to characterize who and what you are to me. You both have so much faith in me that at times it makes me nervous. I had to quickly realize that you saw what I could not see in myself. You both are the best parents this girl could ever ask for. This book is a product of your amazing demonstration of love, patience, and support. Thank you for loving me as your own.

My bonus mom Aleyda, you are literally one of my best friends and teacher. Thank you for preaching me back to my senses. Thank you for all of your thought-provoking conversations that inspired me to get the help I needed to change. You constantly remind me of my greatness. I am grateful for our late-night conversations and you accompanying me in my moments of distress.

To the most awesome siblings William and Keysha Hall, you both are my backbone; I cannot even use "in- laws". Thank you for your support and your selfless acts of kindness.

To Will and Inga Brown, Shayla and Ramon Hamilton, life would not be the same without your guidance and support. Life would not be the same without you—the family I have always wanted.

To my brother Malik, I could not ask for a better God father to my children and friend. You have been constant in my life through my highs and lows; thank you for giving me a sister in Sheree.

To my Gramma Ella Hamilton, you were my number one cheerleader. No matter what I was doing, you were right there pushing me. I am sorry you did not get this book in time to read it, but you live on in my heart.

To the women of faith pillars in my life, Jane Hendrickson, Vivian Harvey, Myrtle Purdue, Martha Thompson, Tina Nelson, and Sharon Thompson, these years have been nothing short of eventful and I am grateful you were there to pray me through.

I am blessed to have awesome sisters Shayla Hamilton, Lashay McKnight, Dawn Garrick ,and Brianna Naves, who over the years have been my partners in prayer and wise counsel. You all are amazing women of God who have been in my lows and highs. Thank you for giving room to fail and grow.

To my girls Jennifer Alline and Deborah Moore, you both are such amazing vessels who have blessed my life through your passion and genuineness. Our college adventures were so great, that twelve years later we are still riding this wave together. Thank you for being consistent with me over the years and understanding me.

Leah and Lauren, my God daughters you are beautiful bundles of Joy that I enjoy sharing my life with. I look forward to seeing you grow because you are both my inspiration. I love you!

Mehaylia Ramsey, you are such a dynamic woman of Elohim. I am so grateful to have you as a friend and sister. We spend hours laughing and conversing about different angles to scripture. You are such an inspiration. Thank you for believing in me and sowing into my life.

Pastor Joshua Selma, as I fasted your sermons helped awaken me and provided me with so much clarity. I hope I can meet you one day soon.

Cherry Williams, also known as mama Cherry, thank you for your words of wisdom. I am so grateful that God allowed our paths to cross. You embraced me as a daughter. You prayed for me and corrected me when you were prompted. I will never forget your kindness. You challenged me to confront the issues that I held in my heart for so long. Thank you for helping me properly mourn my father's death after 11 years of suppressing the hurt it caused. Thank you for teaching me how to better my relationship with my mother. Thank you for taking your valuable time with a stranger by investing your gifts into my life and requesting nothing in return but my healing.

In this season, God has not ceased to amaze me how the puzzle pieces in my life have fallen into place and you Pastor Belinda John are one of them. Our destinies just crashed into each other during the most pivotal time of my life. You are one of those benefits that I can partake of being the daughter of a King whose desire for my life is wholeness. Dr. Belinda you are one of heavens greatest counselors and teachers. You gave me an ear to listen and a shoulder to cry on. I could not write this book without thanking you for the love, patience, and the grace you have showed me. Thank you for adopting me and caring for me as the effective leader that you are. Thank you for your sage correction and your prayers. When I think about you, I think about the word "balance". You came into my life to teach me how to be a balanced wholesome woman of God. I cannot express how thankful I am for you. God knew exactly what I needed when I was at a crossroad in my life and you came into it. I know that God will reward your works.

INTRODUCTION

You are a portable power supply—the lifeline of this modern world and of the generations to come. In Salvation University, you learn the schematics needed to nurture your battery, increase your charge, and operate at peak condition. A well-powered battery provides direct accessibility to the governor of your power supply. Therefore, once adequately powered, you are able to better communicate with God. This is where you can more clearly see the blueprint for your life. You can see directly into the realms that obstruct the proper flow of your power.

Batteries are used in a variety of devices, some large and some small; however, the main function of a battery remains the same, which is to provide power. We are all different batteries from various walks of life, but our main function is to provide power to the world around us by fulfilling our God-designed purposes. Some of us are powered for battles, others are powered to intercede or intercept, but either way—we are required to be a charge. It does not matter on which side you stand; a battle must be fought nonetheless. The goal here is to utilize the strategies examined during our courses at Salvation University in order to win the war so that we can experience the benefits of being triumphant.

Countless exams I have failed. Some exams I have had the opportunity to retake. Every time I have had to redo those tests, I've learned something new. However, one thing remained constant, which was God's unwavering love for my wavering heart. Hard knocks may be the name to all my bumps and bruises, but I have overcome and so can you.

Thank you for coming on this exploratory journey. To enjoy the process of self-discovery and be empowered by the spirit of these words. If you are anything like me, you need a book that helps awaken your senses. A book that acts as a navigation assistant through the desolate unaddressed highways of your mind and one that helps to reconfigure the desires of your heart.

May you find clarity within this book and the necessary charge to power your battery. I have had the pleasure of finding books at the right seasons of my life to help steer me through some courses at Salvation University and I pray that this book will be the catalyst to propel you to the next dimension of your life.

CHAPTER ONE

A WELL-POWERED BATTERY

A battery, in general terms, is a device that stores chemical energy by converting it to electrical energy. The chemical reactions involved in a battery are electrons from one material, electrode to another through an external circuit. These flowing electrons in turn provide an electric current that is used to do work. Now, you are wondering why am I talking about batteries? What relevance does this have in the bigger scheme of life? My response is "plenty"!

If you understand how a battery is used, charged, and protected you will understand the parallelism of its function to life and your own life force. If you begin to see yourself as a device that either holds or loses a charge, you will recognize imminent danger when surrounded by people who deplete your battery's power. I must mention that batteries discharge and that is a natural phenomenon. With the busyness of life and the trials that we face, it is expected that our batteries will, at times, lose charge. Therefore, it is imperative to be plugged into the proper connection because this determines the life span and the power supply of our internal battery.

⚡ BATTERY LIFE

Note that I am not simply personifying a battery and explaining to you what it does. I am telling you that your spirit is your battery and it is important to know what powers it. We are told that our bodies give life to our spirit; but on the contrary it is our spirit that gives life to our bodies. This earthly temple also known as a vessel can be described as the machine whose machinery is dependent on the power received through a battery to function. Our faith is the flow of the electrical current that is used to do work. Work is what you were designed to do. Your purpose in life is your work. In the beginning, when God created heaven, earth, and all features that we gloriously partake in, it says he "worked" and then ceased from working. We are introduced to this concept of "work" in the formation of this universe so that we can understand that God placed his energy into purpose. We are functional beings created and crafted by a functional father who worked to perfect every detail within us.

> *"When you refuse to work, you deny yourself the opportunity to fulfill your purpose"* -Dr. Myles Munroe

In physics, the term "work" is an energy transfer due to displacement of an object. Therefore, to receive the manifestation of our purpose, we must put our hands to the plough which is work. Your electrochemical potential is worth nothing unless it is being used; therefore, put into motion. It is our faith that provides the charge we need to effectively do work.

> *"But do you want to know, O foolish man, that faith without works is dead."* -James 2:20 (NKJV)

When you are operating at peak condition, you realize that your powered battery requires a level of faith to keep its power. There is a mutualistic relationship between work and faith. One cannot exist without the other. They both must synergistically function in unison.

> *"And without faith it is impossible to please God"*
> *-Hebrews 11:6 (NIV).*

The rest of the verse lets us know that we must come with faith to God and he in turn will reward those who diligently seek him. In order to diligently seek God, there is a level of displacement that must occur on our behalf. In other words, I must have faith in the energy I am placing in chasing after God. I must transfer a certain amount of energy, my life force into looking for God so that I can receive a reward.

At different seasons of our lives we can miss parts of this mutualistic relationship between faith and work. At times, our faith capacitor is not firing at its intended capacity, and our work can become a hindrance to our faith. For me, I was missing the Faith part of the equation. I was missing the portion that cries, "come with belief". I was too frustrated doing "work" that the reward I received was not fulfilling. The direction of my life did not equate to the work I did. Not having my prayers answered in the way I believed they should have took an immense toll on my faith. As my faith dwindled, so did my trust in God's capability. I was praying from a place of worry rather than coming to God fueled with faith. Therefore, no matter how much I worked, my frustration overpowered my faith leaving me feeling powerless, doubtful, and ultimately in disbelief. I also realized I was not plugged into the proper circuits to power charge my battery.

One day, I was working on my computer and its battery was dying. I plugged my computer in every electrical socket in the living room. I figured if the sockets were being used, nothing could be wrong with them. I thought there must be something wrong either with the charger or the computer. For weeks, I

⚡ **BATTERY LIFE**

struggled to charge my computer in my living room. I was blowing into the computer's battery port like a cartridge from an old Nintendo game in hopes for it to work. I was thinking maybe it had dust accumulating inside of it. I positioned and repositioned the battery on the floor, on the table, and on the couch. However, once I found a sweet spot; It would charge for a minute or two and then stop charging. In urgency one day, I ran to my room and plugged the charger because I needed to submit my work. Lo and behold, my computer charger light turned right on and began to charge. It finally dawned on me that the problem was not the computer or the charger, but the electrical sockets. It was hard for me to believe it was the sockets in the living room because they were powering other devices that I use in my home. However, the power flowing from the socket to my computer was not sufficient to provide a consistent charge. The same happens to our spiritual battery. Just because we see other people plugged into certain connections and thriving, it does not mean that we too can be powered by those same sources. If you are not plugged into proper sockets, you will not have enough power to supply charge to your battery and fulfill your God given assignment. Faith is the catalyst that propels you into different dimensions of grace and favor. It begins a chain reaction to obtain a desired end in the same way a chemical reaction does.

FAITH IS THE POWER KEY TO OUR IMAGINATION.

However, in order to unleash the full power of your faith, you must first remove any cultural, physical, mental, and spiritual limitations. Have you asked yourself how deep or how wide is the sky? Has anyone been able to conceptualize a numeric value for the size of the sky? We have numerical values for the size of the earth also known as a constant, but why not the sky? Many scientists have not been able to agree on where to begin or limit the measurements of the sky. This celestial sphere and many can dispute and say that it is flat shaped or dome shaped; however, this abstract earthly realm contains mysteries that have yet to be solved. The answers are only found where God dwells. These answers are dispensed in increments and can only be obtained in the secret place. Therefore, to receive the understanding of these mysteries your battery must operate at optimal condition; the same goes for your imaginative power. Tapping into your imagination takes a battery that is not encumbered and fully dependent on its source of power. Our imagination is limitless! The composition of our battery contains different elements that allows your earthly device to function and faith is one of them.

Remember, faith can be cultivated by those around us. Those of kindred spirits!

> *"They were all with one mind in one place"*
> *-Acts 2:1b (KJV)*

Understanding that like-minded people who are in God can effectively power charge your battery so that you can be the best version of yourself. The manifestation of God's power was endowed to those who were on the same wavelength so to say. Therefore, receiving what God designed for them, so that they could be connected to the power supply of life on the earth. Time and time again we see the benefits behind the power of connection.

> *"For the promises is to you and your children, and to all who are afar off, as many as the Lord our God will call"*
> *-Acts 2:39 (KJV)*

It was the power of connection that allowed Jesus's body to be wrapped in clean linen and laid in a new tomb (Matthew 27: 57). According to scripture, it was a rich man who was a disciple of Jesus that commanded his body to be released. What kind of influence did this man have? I cannot go to a hospital and command a fellow comrade's body to be relinquished to me because I said so.

Can you imagine the type of power and authority I would need in order to demand from a hospital the corpse of a non-relative? How effective is your battery with the proper connections? Understanding the elements at work within our battery helps give a greater definition of who we truly are in this dimension of life. We have yet to tap into the full power that dwells within our battery.

As you continue to read these pages, you will notice many patterns which are highlighted throughout the bible. I pray these words come alive and ignite your engine. My hope is that you will reflect deep within yourself so that you are empowered to move in God's desired direction for your life. That you will begin to ask yourself questions that will uncover the basis of your beliefs and expose any lies that have held you captive and impede the fulfillment of your purpose. Your destiny is your destination and it hinges on the balance of having a battery that is fully powered and equipped for work.

CHAPTER TWO

BATTERY COMPOSITION

Electricity can neither be caught nor stored, but it is housed within the chemicals inside of a battery. Likewise, within the cell membranes of our physical bodies, the difference in concentration of ions produces an electrical currency which is fueled by ATP (Adenosine triphosphate). Long word right! ATP is produced in the mitochondria and it is used to burn glucose (sugar) and oxygen. It is our membrane's battery, so to say.

    I know what you are thinking this is a spiritual book and not a Biology lesson. However, just go on this trip with me. The body is a storehouse of electricity which is trapped in chemicals in this case, ATP, and then utilized to do work, i.e. function. Our spiritual battery operates much the same way. Our physical bodies are the outer casing used to contain our spiritual battery which produces power (an electrical current) to fulfill our purpose on the earth. We are charged particles in the form of beings created to produce energy for work.

    The main components found within a battery are two terminals which are plates typically made of different compositions also known as current conductors, the electrodes (anode and cathode), and the terminal separator, the electrolyte.

The core components of our spiritual battery are Faith, Trust, and Hope. In other words, these are the electrons that flow and power charge our batteries .

They are the building blocks of our salvation that provide us with the benefits of being in the kingdom of God. In turn we experience God's gifts, the manifestation of his spiritual fruits, and talents from the core elements of our battery. For instance, our faith empowers us to be more like Christ. This allows the fruit of the Spirit to transform our inner beings, but it all begins with faith.

We proclaim the legitimacy of our paternal bond with God, becoming joint heirs with Christ, through the act of salvation. Through this process, we are entitled to become fully charged capacitors divinely enabled to do the intended work that God designed for us from the foundation of time.

For you to believe, you must trust that which you believe. Our confession of faith, although not always obvious, is due to an encounter with God; therefore, that encounter gives you grounds to trust and hope in your profession of faith. I believed in God, but I had no trust in him. Therefore, the premise of trust was nullified because of my lack of faith. The idea of trusting God seemed theoretically sound because I was a believer; however, the truth was that I did not trust God. When my faith was tested, I had to put my faith to practice thus "work" my faith. Rather than believing whole heartedly; I crumbled at the sight of the test. I wondered why it was so difficult for me to be stable in faith and believe in God's ability to see me through the different seasons of my life. I eventually realized that my lack of trust in my heavenly father stemmed from my inability to trust my earthly father. I did not trust God, because I was disappointed in my father. My father failed me and subconsciously I believed

God would fail me too. I felt like my father had not properly prepared me for life. I felt abandoned and I was left with countless unanswered questions. I was disappointed in the decisions my father made which led to his untimely departure. Imbued in that disappointment, I began to unknowingly weld my father's characters and shortcomings with God. Placing them both in the box of unreliability, disappointment, disgust, and hatred. If you are wondering if I walked away from my faith, I did not. Instead, I became a well-polished pretender. I placed layers and layers of masks upon my faith. I continued to smile and pretend so that I could forget the real root of the contagion. Visiting old wounds seemed far more dangerous and overwhelming than creating healed portraits of myself. No one needed to know that I was hurting, and I did not have to admit that to myself. I knew I loved God; I was still in church and so I thought this was enough to get me by. The issue here is that salvation encompasses a greater depth of understanding of oneself so that a mutual relationship with God can be established. However, I used God as a distraction and not as a solution. I hear people often say, "fake it until you make it." There is such irony and danger to this quote, because you can fake it so much, that you actually begin to believe the fallacies.

    However, what happens when "faking it" goes awry? Faking requires lots of energy and in turn you use that energy to mask and create more layers to cover our disappointments and internal baggage. This is where "faking" becomes dangerous! I placed layers to my faith, and I masked the layers of unforgiveness on my face. This bled into my marriage, all of my relationships, and even into my parenting. **The issues we have with God are sometimes a collection of baggage; the things that we will not admit to ourselves.** God cannot take from us our hurt, our traumas, and our failures if we do not give him those painful experiences. Handing over requires humbleness, and a certain level of maturity. This is where the term "work" comes into play. This is a level of displacement that must occur on our behalf so that our battery can function at its intended capacity. At the time humility and maturity were not ingredients I was willing to use.

"He leads the humble in what is right and teaches the humble his way" -Psalms 25:9

I was so accustomed to shelving the spices in my faith that I did not understand I was actually shelving the issues I was not willing to acknowledge. Culturally speaking, I was taught masking is the solution to any disease. You can clap, dance, and forget all about your problems, no one needs to know about your issues, and you cannot trust anyone including yourself. We are pre programmed to believe that we are an island and that internalizing our experiences is the best solution for dealing with the issues that flow out of our heart. As if communication were not a key ingredient in our survival and salvation.

In the garden of Eden, there was communication between man and God, but more importantly there was utter dependency on God. Therefore, trust was established from the beginning. God trusted Adam and Eve with the Garden and gave them parameters not to breach. God would not give you a responsibility if he did not trust you. God enjoyed conversation so much that when his trust was violated, he called to Adam and asked "Where are you?" (Genesis 3:9)

God could have yelled his name and said, "Adam what have you done?" or even obliterated them from existence. I can count the many times my parents allowed me to explain myself. Other times, they reacted out of the sheer anger caused by my disobedience. Now, that I am a mother I better relate to how my parents felt. Understanding that parenting is not always about reactivity, but rather reasoning. I have allowed God to rewire my conditioning and adopted his philosophy of conversing with my children rather than going straight for punishment. God was introducing His concept of conversation and communication. Let us talk through this infraction so that you can understand the sentencing you are going to receive.

Do you not think that God knew where Adam was if he has a bird's eye view of the earth, let alone the Garden?

But You are He who took Me out of the womb; You made Me trust while on My mother's breasts. -Psalm 29: 9

See, our dependency on God was ingrained in us from within the womb. We were being conditioned to physically accept what was already endowed to us spiritually. How does a child trust that their parent will hold them up in their arms and not drop them? I had this epiphany with my first born. Every time he extended his hands as a sign for me to hold him, he did not think to himself my mother would drop me. If that were the case, he would not have his hands outstretched towards me. His reach was an act of trust that I would be the one to hold him and allow him to see the world from where I stood.

Can you see the world from where God stands? First, you have to let God hold you so that you can get a better view. We are already pre-programmed as God's creation to trust. When we are children, our trust and faith capacitor is operating at optimal condition because it has not been tainted by external factors.

"Assuredly, I say to you unless you are converted and become as little children, you will by no means enter the kingdom of heaven. -Matthew 18:3

This idea to become as little children allowed me to see God as my children see me. That as God is a well of power fully fortified by faith, trust, and hope... so am I.

Unfortunately, as adults we resort to the blame game, making God the enemy of our scars, when the real blame lies in the well-covered sin within us.

Charge interruptions usually begin during the most impressionable or vulnerable times of our lives, which can be either during childhood or adulthood. For me, my charge was intercepted as a child, and as an adult. Due to the faults within my battery, I operated at sub-par conditions for far too long.

When we are challenged in our relationships, parenting, or in different areas of our lives, that is when we can clue into whether we are plugged into the right power source. When we are not fully aligned with the Word of God as our power source, we allow ourselves to become haughty, indignant, and defensive and then we cleverly cloak it all with self-righteousness.

As we bleed internally, we hurt those around us unaware of the real cause of our infectious nature. There are trials, that if you allow them to, will harden your heart. You must be aware of this! It is our defense mechanisms that create the layers around the core of our battery by preventing us from experiencing similar hurts again. Sometimes these raw materials hinder our ability to get to the root of the matter if we do not dig deep enough to find those deficiencies. When your heart is hardened, it constricts the flow of the set apart spirit; therefore, draining the life in your battery. These faults can cause a bottleneck effect. By the time you notice the issues operating at large, you no longer can identify who you are. It is like placing a noose on your neck and the longer your feet are without ground the less ability you have to breath until you die. This is what lack of trust will do to your faith; it will smite it. Countless times the scriptures mention trusting in God.

Blessed is the man who trusts in the Lord
-Jeremiah 17:7.

We see that trust is a core element encompassed within our battery. The reason we struggle to face the issues in our hearts, is because we become professional painters; attempting to recreate formulations from the unacknowledged fragmented pieces of ourselves. There is nothing wrong with rewriting our story; however, we must revisit and heal the person we were in the past chapters of our lives, in order to become the best version of ourselves in the present. **It makes absolutely no sense to paint over a broken vessel, because it simply does not erase the brokenness.** In fact, the more we paint, the more visible the cracks show. This was a difficult concept for me to grasp, because I thought I was a new creature.

He who is in Christ is a new creature.
-2 Corinthians 5:17

I acknowledged who I was, but I thought I did not have to delve into my past because my past had been forgotten and forgiven by God. I could slightly trust God with the present me, but I could not trust him with my past—as if He did not see the story unfold. I did not think the past me needed reconciliation with the present me. What a deception to walk in! It was not only dangerous for myself, but also for those who were around me. I thought if I could fix myself now, there was no reason to revisit old scars. Healing comes by way of admittance, which includes visiting the desolate areas in our lives.

The survival of your battery is contingent on your utter reliance on God. This includes trusting him to rewire your battery and stabilize the layers that protect your core. All which are directly involved in the transference of those electron ions that power your battery. Remember, those faults left unchecked, only interfere with your electrical current's ability to produce power; so it is imminent to address them all.

⚡ **BATTERY LIFE**

We cannot allow our brokenness to dictate our relationship and view of God. If we do, we leave ourselves open to falling into pits of despair and desolation. I have been on a roller coaster ride believing one minute and doubting the next. The more time I spent on that ride the more anxious and tired I became. The pits looked larger and deeper by the minute. I was like a literal wave tossed to and fro at the mercy of every storm I faced. I wondered if God could even reach me where I was, because I was so full of confusion and negativity. There is hope! I can attest that no matter where you are God can find you.

He knew where Adam was in the Garden, and he knows exactly where you are right at this moment. The question that remains is whether you will step outside yourself and have an honest and open conversation with God? David understood this during his times of reflection.

"If I make my bed in hell, behold you are there"
-Psalms 139: 8b

Will you trust God with every part of you in order to find the lost you and allow Him to coach you through the broken places in your life?

For the Son of Man has come to seek and to save that which was lost. -Luke 19:3

Reconciliation is our portion! Trust is removing self-reliability and exalting God's power in his ability above our understanding. Your battery was created by God, so he alone understands how you function and which wires need reprogramming, realignment, and removal.

Trust works in conjunction with faith. In some seasons of our life, our faith ions can dwindle. However, it is those trust ions and hope ions in God that will provide the electrical charge to your inner being and pick up the slack for your battery to be operational.

> *Now faith is the substance of things hoped for, the evidence of things not seen. Hebrews. 11:1*

Like a battery, the ions that flow cannot be visibly seen to the naked eye, so it is with our trust, hope, and faith in God; all which together power our spiritual battery. Now, that you understand and can visualize the main components within your spiritual battery; there are elements that are found within the layers of your battery. These layers are raw materials intended to protect the core of the reactions and generate current to power your device, your battery, or the battery of those around us. However, unlike a battery, our experiences govern the creation of those layers. These layers either allow us to function or they hinder our ability to do work.

As newborns, our batteries operate at optimal condition. We have yet to experience the traumas that psychologically, physically, or spiritually hinder our growth. Newborns are like malleable wires that can be molded at the will of the environment. As we get older and begin to interact with the world those layers within us begin to shape. Depending on those experiences whether positive or negative; the layers within our battery are formed to protect our core and also transfer charge. Our neural highways as newborns, have yet to experience disappointment, failure, regret, doubt, and shame. However, it is the emotional bric-a-brac accumulated from our childhood, adulthood, or a combination of both that creates the heavy burdens which we carry throughout life. The layers in our battery serve as a material storehouse. Living in a delusion of unprocessed waste will impede your progress and momentum for growth. If we do not seek God's intervention, it is those experiences that hinder our beings from thriving and our batteries to be fully functional for use. On this spiritual journey with God, it is the ever-increasing knowledge of our batteries' power that enable us to navigate through our internal turmoil, external traumas, and the personalities that govern our character.

In chemistry, a solution is a homogeneous mixture specifically composed of two or more substances. Prayer, meditation, and fasting are these homogeneous mixtures i.e. solution. It is the electrolyte, which is a chemical medium in our battery. The lubricant for your electrical plates, also known as current conductors.

The electrolyte allows both metals to break down into ions and allows the electrons to provide electricity, our ability to power and function. Without this mixture our battery would not be functional because the supply of power would be interrupted.

The key components which power the basic functionality and properties within your battery are prayer, meditation, and fasting. Prayer is the material used for the electrodes and the electrolyte which is where reactions occur within your battery. What do I mean? Prayer is the electrolyte which is the chemical medium where transfers of electrons take place. This transfer I speak of are our petitions which is the dialogue between God and yourself. It is the spiritual battlefield; the push and pull in our salvation, the heart of the chemical reaction is this solution. Fasting and meditation are the other substances within the mixture of the electrolyte in your battery. It is the reaction medium which lubricates your prayers to unhinderedly get God's attention. Where we engage in spiritual warfare thus the location where reactions within the spiritual realm take place.

The plates on a battery are negative or positive, depending on the active material they hold. Thus these two terminals are made of different chemicals. In this case, the holy spirit is the negative plate and the flesh, the extension of this human body is the positive plate. You are probably wondering why I would use negative for the spirit and positive for the flesh? Does this not sound counter intuitive? Yes, it is! These electrical plates are the current conductors within our battery, also opposing factors. In order to facilitate electron transfers in the form of current, these two plates are submerged in the electrolyte, solution composed of prayer, fasting and meditation.

    The Holy Spirit, being the negative terminal (anode), will break down into ions within us which then produce God's spiritual fruits. This in turn yields into electricity, the current used to supply our battery's life. The negative ions are those that participate in the charging scheme of your battery. This positive plate, cathode contributes to electrons flowing to discharge. However, when charging a cell, the cathode becomes the negative electrode. What does this mean? Depending on your potential to charge or discharge will determine your ability to provide the electrical power to work.

    Will you be charged by the spirit or discharged by the flesh?

For the flesh lusts against the Spirit, and the Spirit against the flesh; and these are contrary to one another, so that you do not do the things that you wish. -Galatians 5: 17

SUPER CHARGE PRAYER

Father teach me how to function at optimal condition. As you father give knowledge and skill in all learning and wisdom according to Daniel 1: 17, I ask that you endow me with your skills. That I may apply knowledge, wisdom, and learning in all areas of my life. Show me the faults and the deficiencies within my battery. I desire for my spiritual battery to be unhindered in my supply of power from you. I no longer want to be encumbered with any childhood or adulthood traumas that will hinder my ability to fulfill my purpose. Jesus said not one stone will be left upon another, that will not be thrown down (Mark 13:2). Show me the stones in my life that need to be uncovered. Any stony layers within my heart father, I now give you permission to tear them down. I acknowledge that I need you to expose the desolate areas that I am afraid to revisit. Strip me of any lies that have held me imprisoned from experiencing your freedom.

Father, I bless your name because you are my rock. According to Psalm 144: 1 you are the one who trains my hand for war and my fingers for battle. Thank you for teaching me your ways, so that my spiritual battery can effectively do its intended work, which is to power the world around me so that the world may glorify you. I ask all of these things in the name of the set apart one, our messiah, Jesus Christ. Amen.

CHAPTER THREE

SELECTING A RECHARGING STATION

At times we can unknowingly permit distractions to drain our batteries. When drained, we function much like pressure cookers—just waiting to burst at any moment. We can allow the pressures of life, through our limited perceptions of time and people's opinions, to dictate the course and the direction of our sail. Have you ever asked yourself *"who governs the current in the ocean?"*

Scientifically, the ocean is governed by a synergic relationship between the ocean's wavelength, water depth, and gravity. Spiritually speaking our own current is governed by the depth of our relationship with God; intimacy becomes the gravitational mass that pulls us closer to the source of our power. It is your ability to trust *the creator of the current* so that you will not fall into the trap of prematurely making decisions that can adversely affect various areas of your life.

So fully trusting in God, includes patiently waiting on God. Waiting, although challenging at times, allows our endurance meter to grow. Waiting purifies our motives. Waiting can seem like torment if you have not given yourself entirely to the process. It is falling in love with the process that allows you to see the benefits of waiting, because in due time you will be able to run.

> *But they that wait upon the LORD shall renew their strength; they shall mount up with wings as eagles; they shall run, and not be weary; and they shall walk, and not faint*
> *-Isaiah 40:31.*

I wonder how many people have noticed this scripture emphasizes running first before walking. Why is that? Do we not walk before we run? This would be my rationalization too! Being on my emotional roller-coaster ride with God, not being able to hear God through all my clutter did not allow me to even see the word "run". I was too focused on being weary. This scripture mentions running first because we run to our desired end, so that we can walk the rest of the journey. The running allows us to make up for the time we thought we lost. God is the commander and chief of time.

> *The author and the finisher of our faith. -Hebrew12:2*

He is an author, the writer of our novel. He is a finisher the one who will complete our novel; therefore, what he starts he fulfills.

> *Do not turn to the right or the left. -Proverbs 4:27*

This is an instructional verse. When running, you have no time to look to the right or the left but straight ahead. During the "wait' it allows your motives to be purified. This will eliminate you from being distracted by various temptations that can obstruct your forward propellent. Those hindrances that impede your speed and arrival to the fulfillment of your purpose and destiny so that you can walk the rest of the journey. It gives you the opportunity hon into your purpose. To become strong and exercise your "discipline". Proverbs 4:13 reads *"Hold on to instruction"*. What were you instructed to do? Your instruction is your discipline. An alternate version of proverbs 4:13 says *"Become strong in discipline, do not let it go; watch over her for she is your life"*.

You need discipline over your life! Your instruction, to be disciplined, is the blueprint to your destination. It is that strong pull that requires your attention. Once your motives are purified, (demonstrated by your willingness to heed instructions) then, and only then does the real race begins. We can obtain everything we thought was delayed while running so that we can then walk out our purpose, our instruction, and our discipline with purity of heart.

Waiting enables our batteries to be fully recharged. It allows us to reconnect with the source of our power so that we have enough energy to work, run, and fulfill our God given assignments.

Once we understand that our batteries need recharging, waiting seems less daunting. We can surrender more fully to the pruning process of waiting. It is our ability to exercise care for our battery's life that keeps it's power flowing uninterruptedly. So, waiting allows us to be both processed and silenced.

We live in a world that is constantly evolving and can easily be swept up by the feeling to need to keep busy. The pressure of needing to belong and having a purpose can at times interfere with the waiting process causing us to become too distracted to listen. I was too busy trying to make my life make sense that I was not busy enough honing my discipline. I allowed the riff-raff in my life to determine what was acceptable at the

⚡ BATTERY LIFE

time. We live in a culture where busyness is glorified, yet it is that same busyness which renders us unable to listen to the set apart spirit of God.

Christopher Reeves, best known as superman, once said "I think we all have a little voice inside us that will guide us… If we shut out all the noise and clutter from our lives and listen to the voice, it will tell us the right thing to do." He was truly on to something here! Noise pollution can come in various forms, silencing our inner voice, thus rendering our hearing useless. We are unable to listen to our call, purpose, discipline, or instruction. We are unable to feel or hear our battery draining and sometimes we wait until it is completely drained recharge.

When your battery is completely depleted, your recharging process takes longer; therefore, you are sidelined longer. This creates unnecessary frustration. However, if we learn to notice our battery's power indicators, the process of recharging will seem less unsettling. Recharging your battery may involve moving away from an external power source. The external sources that supply your battery power determine how quickly and effectively your battery is either recharged or drained.

At various junctions in our salvation, our battery will need different charging schemes just like different battery chemistries. These strategies help you navigate through the blueprints laid out for that particular chapter in your life. During our waiting period, this allows the noise pollution to cancel out, so that we can have clarity of our assignments and instructions. Many of us are frustrated, tired, and have stopped dreaming because we cannot hear our call to purpose. Some of us have aborted the mission too soon because the wait was too long. Others do not know where to begin to make the appropriate applications of change because we have become, so accustomed to the mundane responsibilities and limitations around us. Sometimes our own failures and the cries of those disappointments are pollutants that cloud our judgment. They percolate the doubt clouds reeving havoc in our minds and in turn we ignore what is true and great possibilities we can experience. Frustration will reduce the power in your battery instantly. For so long, I asked God to show me the direction and path I should take. The truth is I did not want to listen. Many of us do not want to listen or do not know how to listen. I was too focused on being frustrated and weary. I was afraid that God would tell me that my pursuits were purely self-gratifying. Everything from work to school seemed so mundane. I hated my very existence because I felt and I knew that there was more to my life. I could not put my finger exactly where this discontent came from—all I knew is that I was not satisfied. The idea of me becoming a physician theoretically made sense; it was great. I knew it would make my mother proud and the financial stability was also a benefit. I was molded to believe that only certain careers were worthy of praise and anything else meant nothing. Never would I have thought writing would be an outlet that God would use to exercise my training, because that was not what I thought I wanted. I definitely did not think that God wanted this for me either. I was not ready to admit that those dreams were imposed on me. That they infringed upon everything that brought me joy—writing being one of them. As time passed, I realized I only wanted this paper as a validation to my intelligence. It would assure me of being a good daughter and I would be validated in my mother's eyes for following *her* dreams. See, the validation from a human being, my mother, my family, and friends, at that time, were greater for me than the validation and fulfillment of my calling to God. There was no real happiness in that. I had to soon realize that this doctorate would be more for my mother so that she could gloat and say her daughter is a medical doctor, while I died on the inside living without my real purpose. Waiting allowed me to dig deep and listen to the nuggets of wisdom available to me in the silence.

I put aside all the busyness in my mind. I was able to abandon what I thought I wanted in order to explore the combination of God-given talents that would bring me joy. That would allow me to fulfill my actual purpose.

I have found that very few people tap into and execute their real and preordained purpose. Instead we allow our culture, people, situations, and time to determine our pursuit of purpose and do not give God half the courtesy to jump in faith.

"One evening, after yet another of his magnificent concerts, world renowned pianist Van Cliburn was approached by an admirer who had been in the audience. Obviously touched by the performance the emotional fan grasped Cliburn's hand and said: "I would give my life to be able to play the piano like that." The pianist smiled and replied, "I DID."

My deepest desire was to give my life to live my life. I want to relay to my children and those that came after that I gave my life to find and live through my purpose.

If *you* are not in the designed lane which was established for *you* from the foundation of the time, *you* cannot come into the fullness of God's benefits for *your* calling. Therefore, something will always be missing. Waiting allowed me to dismantle the walls that were hindering my call and tackle areas of my life that I did not want to hand over to God. I guess the load was easier to bare than to face God and face myself. Waiting allowed me to ingest the wisdom that forced my hands to crash into my purpose.

God will allow you to endure the process of waiting to get your attention, make you listen and make a product that only he can get the glory for.

Can you say that you have waited the process in silence to utterly understand your purpose so that you can fulfill what only you were designed to do?

Joseph had to experience "waiting" and underwent a purification process to be a vessel in deliverance for his family and a community. Joseph's trajectory was a roller coaster of events from being sold into slavery by his brothers for having a vison, to being imprisoned for having integrity. If you are on ones of those roller coaster, Fret not! How much time lapsed before Joseph become the second most powerful man in Egypt? Could we say that if anyone could be tired it would be Joseph. What conversation was Joseph having within himself? What if Joseph allowed the noise pollution of complaints due to the injustice he faced to interfere with his purpose? Where would his family be? Where would Pharaoh be? If you are wondering why Pharaoh, his dream was the catalyst in revealing the power of God in Joseph. Famine would have struck Pharaohs house and he would not have known what hit him. Even here, we notice God's mercy for the overlord. God allowed Pharaoh to experience his grace because God was truly saving Israel from famine. This is the power of connection working at large.

Waiting builds character! Through this charter building block Joseph was processed so that he could be a benefit to an entire nation.

Has your faith in God wavered because the process has been prolonged longer than you imaged? Is your faith wavering because your prayers are not being answered? I can list a couple of events in history where people had to wait and be pruned to accomplish Gods intensions. The waiting process truly shows what you are truly made of. The children of Israel were Captive in Egypt for 430 years.

Now the sojourn of the children of Israel who lived in Egypt was four hundred and thirty years. -Exodus 12:40.

Can you imagine being trapped that long in a wilderness of despair?

They waited 430 years for a vessel, Moses to appear on their behalf and aid in their deliverance. Then, spent 40 Years in a desert (Neh9:21) but their shoes never wore out (Deut29:5). During the pruning process, the Israelites needed to refine the core elements in their battery, trust, hope, and faith in God. This allowed a separation between the complainers, faithless, hopeless, and trustless. When you cannot get your way, what conversations do you have with God, yourself, and those around you?

What comes out of the mouth, this defiles and man.
-Matthew 15:11b

Are you defiling who God created you to be because of the words you are allowing to take root in your heart? After failing multiple tests at Salvation University, did I finally understand the concept of waiting. Words mold your now and your future!

Word are elements found within your battery. Just as Lithium is an element in the periodic table and used in rechargeable batteries so are words. A combination of words are compounds. When these compounds, words are broken down, they act as catalyst that charge the atmosphere in your favor or directly oppose you. Words are so powerful you were created by them so never diminish its power and run from those who do.

My husband used to get on my case about the things I said when I did not get my way. I thought this was him attacking my character and he did not understand why I felt the way I did. I paid for my pious indignation. The truth is that I was so wrapped in myself that I did not pay attention to the words I was speaking over my life out of mere frustration. I was literally orchestrating my own demise. I called myself fat and I got fat.

I said this is taking too long, what else Lord. It took longer. After waiting seven years to understand what God was saying to me through him, my mentor said the same thing. Finally, a light bulb went off in my mind and I realized that I needed to rewire my thinking process because my survival depended on it. I quickly understood that I needed to enjoy the growing pains rather than complain because it would only sharpen my blade.

You can either allow the waiting process to make you a complainer and in turn reduce the power flowing through your battery or you can increase its potential by recharging your battery along the wait.

I believe that if the people of God thanked him for the process their sojourn in the desert would have been less. If they understood that character would allow them to manage the land that God would give them. God cannot take you into your promise land with a distorted view of who he is when the pressure of life is upon you. This pressure determines the shape that you will take from.

Therefore, many perished and could not even give an account of what God had done. -Numbers 14:29

Are you willing to die with all the gifts God has given you? To die not leaving a print of Gods power on the earth for those after you, due to your lack of maturity. They could not partake in the Glory of being free to recreate a new life for their lack of patience and gratitude. Patience, endurance and gratitude are electrical ions that work to increase your battery's performance. Is it not your desire to be free and bask in the glory of God?

Sometimes, obtaining the glory take times. During their wait, they did not allow faith, hope and trust to increase the meter of gratitude or endurance. It is imperative to have gratitude which is a core component in character. Their shoes not wearing out and constant provision was not enough evidence to endure the process of waiting. When my husband and I got married, he was 23 and I was 22 years old. We had no financial stability and a future full of possibilities with so many unknown variables. I am accustomed to controlling everything. I admit I am a bit of a control freak which is extremely opposed to Faith. The unknown variables of not being able to pay our rent on time or even have a car that was our own, created so much tension and distress to our marriage. Despite the eviction notice being on our door and God coming through for us at the eleventh hour was not enough consolation for me. The fact that his parents had a spare vehicle for us to use, was not enough for me either. The fact that we did not go one day without eating organic Greenwise chicken was not enough. I realized I was just as the Israelites. I murmured without cause. I was contentious and angry. I was unable to thank God for the provision in my life and for him coming through time and time again. Frustration can overpower your ability to see provisions as you wait. Ungratefulness is the prerequisite for being locked out of the promises that God has ordained for you. Your character is the foundation to your office. God cannot give you a promotion without you earning it first.

  If you are in the desert, allow your battery to be processed and enjoy the desert. Once you come out the flow of charge flowing through your battery will activate the heavenly host to come down and pave a way for you to thrive. The old behavior and your old way of thinking must die in the desert so that it is not a hindrance in how you govern God's blessing in the promise land.

And they overcame him by the blood of the Lamb and by the word of their testimony, and they did not love their lives to the death.
-Revelation 12:11

    The bloodshed of Christ was not in vain. It was purposeful and strategic. The blood would provide a victory regardless of the rowing seas in front of you. The blood would be guard and a barrier around the fence of your temple where the spirit of God dwells, your battery.

    Overcoming by the word of your testimony encompassed seeing the failures of those in the past. Learning from their mistakes and allowing those mistakes to bear witness in you so that you can utterly relay on God alone. Allow those experiences of old to charge your battery because God does not waiver; he is constant.

For I am the Lord, I do not change. -Malachi 3:6 a

    Do you love your life so much that you are willing to die for it purposeless? Christ died with a purpose and an intention to reconcile Gods creation to his love so that you can power the world as Christ did. Time again we witness God's mercy. Unfortunately, we do not always get it right the first time, so we notice that the Israelites in scripture revisit captivity in Babylon as if Egypt or the desert were not enough.

Then it will come to pass, when seventy years are completed.
- Jeremiah 25: 12

    There is a time that has to pass for completion to a matter. Whether it is a Month, Six months or years either way a time of completion must be fulfilled. Hold on to that. Your time will be completed as you are processed, and the wait will end. Captivity for the Israelites again was due to various infractions towards God. However, who paid for those sins?

I am almost certain that many of them thought "How long Lord" throughout the generations.

The dimension of your calling is reveled over time. If you allow your battery to recharge and wait for the precise "full charge" indicator to appear, you can hone into your discipline and fulfill the assignments you have on the earth. If God just wanted you to exist, you would have remained a spirit in the spiritual realm; there would be no need for your physical body. This tells us that for God to operate he needs a vessel. You are needed! You are essential! However, God desires for you to be fully powered in your physical body and empowered by the spirit so that you can execute his assignment.

There is a God-given purpose only you alone can fulfill
-Belinda John.

Waiting reveals the real composition of your battery. It exposes the defaults found within the core and the layers of our battery. What is the composition of your battery? When pressure is applied, is your powered active or inactive? If your power is active, you will notice that God will lift up standard against the imposters that threaten your destiny. Your battery power will allow you to see with clarity and not scarcity.

What issues within your battery are hindering your ability to be fully charged? During the purifying process, you can identify what you are truly made of. If you only learned to be silent so that you can hear what God is saying. There is a time for completion of everything under the sun. What God allows is for a purpose and a specific time.

I was not able to walk in this insight until now. The

university course of hard knocks, I have failed over the year's countless times. If I can inspire you through my words to avoid those traumatic unnecessary falls, then the failed curriculum was worth all the bruises.

I believe that as supernatural creatures we are endowed with multiple gifting that are found within the layers of our batteries. Those gifts must be processed in the waiting room so that you know how to effectively use them. In the waiting room, you allow the perfecting process to be initiated. The waiting room exposes the inadequacies inside your battery so that you can be reprogrammed, realigned, and repaired. Therefore, once you are in the labor room, you can give birth and run to God's desired end for your life.

RAPID RECHARGE PRAYER

Father, as you are exposing and turning over the stones in my life that encumber my battery; I thank you for my waiting process. During this time, I welcome your wisdom and the strategies I will need to govern your promise land. Thank you for allowing me to wait because once this time is fulfilled; I will be able to run to your desired end for my life. Thank you for giving me rest during the wait. I embrace your peace because you do not give it as the world. Therefore, I will not let my heart be troubled (John 14:27). I will not mummer and waste words. I refuse to defile myself with words that do not align with what you have created and called me to be. I refuse to bare false witness against myself and allow negatively inspired words to condemn and orchestrate my imprisonment. I see myself as you have created me full of potential awaiting to embark on your voyage to greatness. In this process, I will be mindful and superimpose on the old highways in my mind those things that are lovely and of good report. (Philippians 4: 8) I will allow the spirit to produce the necessary fruits so that I can keep the office which you have given me.

Father your word says that the work of righteousness will be peace. (Isiah 32: 17-18) That the effects of righteousness are quietness and an assurance of you forever. I welcome your quietness so that I can hear father what you are saying. Thank you for giving me assurance because my battery dwells in a peaceful habitation. That my vessel is dwelling in safety and I rest in your quietness. In the mighty name of Yeshuah our messiah, your right hand I ask all of these things. Thank you for receiving my prayer. Amen.

CHAPTER FOUR

CORROSION

  A battery corrodes when hydrogen gases are released from the sulfuric acid within a battery. When these gases react to the atmosphere, it produces a corrosive environment. The key word to note here is "within".

  Corrosion is the chemical process of gradual diminution in your battery. It is the cause of an internal conflict. Many of the issues we face in life can produce corrosion within us. Have you become corrosive or allowed corrosive experiences to contaminate your environment? This environment that I speak of is the place where your battery, your spirit dwells.

  Which experiences have shaken your foundation and aided your chemical imbalance? On the spiritual periodic table, Faith, Hope, and Trust are all elements found within. These elemental ions at work in our battery produces the electrical charge to power our being and all that we are capable of producing.

  When this power encompasses gratitude for God's unfailing love and his word, it produces endurance so that our battery can withstand the tests of time and trials. **We were created by words; therefore, words can be found within every fiber of**

our battery's cells. We were created in God's image (Genesis 1:27), so we have the ability to manifest God's characteristics and power. Tapping into God's power is what most of us struggle with.

When we are born, we are like fully charged capacitors. Meaning the composition of our battery is untampered and full of possibilities because it came directly from the creator. As we grow, our experiences begin to challenge and mold who we are at our core. Life experiences can either create limitations by reducing the true potential within your battery or generate endless possibilities. This is where your potential energy crashes into motion thus allowing your battery to do its intended work.

Traumas in life pose a large threat to the functionality of our existence. Traumatic experiences can create toxic internal environments that lessen the lifetime of our batteries. My preferred coping mechanism for stress was food, I wallowed in my sorrow and anger. I walked around with a *woe is me* cloud and basked in the same sorrowful song over and over. I pretended to be okay for so long that I did not notice I was on a slippery slope closer to death than life.

> *A cheerful heart is good medicine,*
> *but a crushed spirit dries up the bones. -Proverbs 17:22*

Is this not cancer that Solomon is referring to when he speaks of the drying of bones? Your desire to live and thrive must be greater than the sorrow and anger you feel. If your bitterness, anger, and hurt are left unchecked, the rifts in your life will seem like enlarging earth fissures. By the time you notice the gaps you would have lost years of your life as well as great relationships in the process. When attempting to weld those gaps with bridges, it will feel like grasping for straws. This is how I felt. I was so lost and held captive in my mind that I could not see God's hand or his power.

> *"If I ascend into heaven, you are there;*
> *if I make my bed in hell, behold you are there. -Psalms 139: 8*

You can be so entrapped in your mind, that life literally feels like hell. God can only enter if you let him in. Holding on to these feelings only further boggles your mind and mental entrapment is corrosive.

When I got married, I gained 50 pounds. You are probably saying I gained "Happy Weight". That was not the case. Gaining weight is just as much physical as it is spiritual. Understating that weight gain is due to mental entanglements is imperative to the overall function of your battery. I was not happy with myself.

Whenever I looked in the mirror, I saw a feeble angry woman. I realized that everything I wanted to accomplish before I got married; I did not have a chance to finish. Not by choice, but because I chose to marry someone my mother did not approve of. It took me getting married to begin to see the real condition of my heart, the real condition of my battery. I realized I had been saved since I was sixteen, but I did not know how broken I was until I was 29 years old. My husband made me happy, but my bitterness ran much deeper than I realized. His love penetrated my hardened heart only but so much. Talk about the basis for issues in a new marriage. I did not notice how broken I was because I kept running and hiding from myself. I was so accustomed to utilizing distractions to ignore my problems. I was distressed and I did not want to be honest with anyone because I was embarrassed. I was judging myself because I placed unrealistic expectations on myself and my marriage suffered for it.

When I began to date my husband, my mother put me out of her house. At the time, she did not approve of him, so she took what I thought was everything. Material things defined me and without them I was nothing. She had my car repossessed on my credit because she paid for it. Can you blame her? She felt that she knew what was best for me. Since I was her dependent, she made sure to not pay for my tuition, nor give me the adequate documentation to continue school. Talk about sabotage! She then began to create stories to justify her actions. She told our family that I left with a drug dealer who was a criminal. The stories we make up in our heads when we do not get our way are fatal to us and those around us. Talk about defamation of character! I had to retake classes for a degree I almost completed because I could not afford private school tuition and get my transcripts. When my father died, he left us with nothing. I had no financial stability. I was unprepared for full adulting when I left her house. I was so angry with my father for leaving me with a mother who did not care to know me. She had her own agenda for my life. I was hurt, and words could not express the turmoil every fiber of my being experienced. I debated starting over and moving far enough where no one could find me. Disappearing for a while seemed like a great solution. I have always been good at running from my problems and layering them with diversions. If you are anything like me, I totally understand! However, those issues amount and collect under layers of pain. What seemed like a frog turns into a dragon. I must say dragons are much harder to slay than frogs.

  At this time, my in laws took me. My mother in-law saw how distressed I was unable to get a job for months that would work around my school schedule. I did not want to drop out for a job. However, it seemed like that was going to be the direction my life was going in. She suggested I go volunteer at the hospital to get me out of the house and distract me. After three days of volunteering, I met an awesome woman who gave me an opportunity and hired me on the spot without experience. Look at God. Did I thank him? "No"! After months of looking for a job,

I was able to land the perfect one by being in position. Although, I was not able to return to private school or get my transcripts because I could not pay the tuition I owed. This job was sent from heaven because it allowed me to go back to school a year later and start over. I was able to go back to school which was so important to me. However, I just kept complaining because the courses I was retaking were a waste of my time. Starting over seemed like such a drag and I was humbled. Overall, I was frustrated that this happened to me because I felt like I had been handed the short end of the stick for no real reason.

    I have always been a pillar of strength to my parents and the fact that they were not that for me seemed unfair. I was saddened because I was my mother's right hand; I did not feel that I deserved this type of reaction from her. I could not understand why it had to be her way or the highway. However, I have learned that my mother's generation is very cut-throat. They give no room for failure and if you fail it is held over your head forever until you have done something substantial to slightly wipe away your wrong. I must take you on a blast into my past so that you can understand the relationship between my mother and I. My father brought me into this country at the age of five. For some reason, the residency cards were only provided to my father and me. I know what you are thinking; they do not separate families. Sometimes they do! It just so happened that we were one of them. I lived with my father and I saw my mother during the summers. There were times when I did not see her for years. Those summer retreats just ended abruptly. I cannot tell you why, but they did.

    For high school, my father dropped me off on my mother's doorstep like a sack of potatoes. I did not know her very well. I spoke with my mother over the phone on the weekends sometimes but there had been no real relationship established. She probably thought she was doing the right thing allowing me to live with my father because everyone in my country was raving about the American educational system. My father was also chasing the American dream. Moving to Florida, I became the errand girl for my mom. I assisted her with everything from helping her in her business to paying all her bills. She really did need the help. See, my mother was an immigrant who came into this country to recreate a life with a family she had already lost; however, she did not know that at the time. To her it seemed as if she could make up for the time that was lost, but it was too late. That must have been truly painful for her and I can see how she assumed she knew what was right for me. However, her expectations of her teenage child strained our relationship. Honesty, I don't think I ever had an opportunity to be a child. I was always taking care of my parents. My mother expected her teenage daughter to know all the American loopholes and ways, which was not the case. However, her lack of trust in me ran deeper than I imagined because she stripped me of everything when she did not get her way. She did not trust that I was mature enough to be with someone she did not choose for me. Her inability to contribute or control my life forced her to give me an ultimatum. I ended up going to a community college and then used those credits to apply to a public university. Despite those small victories, they did not seem like accomplishments to me. The expectations I held for myself trapped me in a box that anything unfamiliar made me cringe. I was too lost in my mind and stuck repeating the same negative events that I was on an insanity roller-coaster ride that I did not know how to get off of. I could not praise or thank God for the opportunity to start over. I was too busy blaming God, my parents, and my husband for the situation, I was in. Time is the ultimate motive purifier because the derailment of my plans helped me find my niche. Although, my mother's intention was to teach me a lesson, life eventually presented me the opportunity to cataclysmically crash into my destiny. Retrospect is always perfect; however, at the time I kept complaining as in my mind the mountains looked lager and closer. The hurdles accumulated and made me angrier and more bitter. I took my anger out on my husband and began to blame him for the journey I was on.

I continually questioned God as to why he had given me the parents he had and what I had done to deserve it all. **I asked all the wrong questions because I was caged in my mind.** My frustration clouded my judgment and fueled my conversations with God. My focus remained on everything that went wrong rather than everything that could go right. I could not see the light at the end of the tunnel because my eyes were closed and fogged by all the pain and disappointment of my past. I have always felt like a misfit, but this was the seal on the coffin. I think my mother thought that by doing all of this I would come running home with my tail between my legs, but I did not. She wanted me to admit that she was right because she felt like she knew what was best for me according to the disappointments she felt. The real issue—which she didn't confront—was not my boyfriend (who is now my husband), but the failed relationship she had with my father. It was the projection of her lack of trust in my father that made her move the way she did towards me. I think that as parents the projection road is a dangerous route to travel because it will cause unnecessary rifts in the relationships we have with our children.

As a result, I felt limited because I was stuck financially, and I had not arrived where I thought I should have been at the time, but I was married. I used to always say "I did things backwards." Are these not negative words that would fulfill themselves in the future some way or somehow? These words would take root in the corners of the earth and produce unprofitable fruit. Corrosive emotions lead to corrosive thinking and result in negative self-fulling prophesies that compromise our destiny.

For as he thinks in his mind, so is he. -Proverbs 23:7

If you do not fill your heart with God's truth, your inner thoughts can cause you to live in delusion forsaking who you are in God.

Their inner thought is that their houses will last forever.
Psalm 49: 11a

When I looked in the mirror, I was the end product of internal acid build up from all the negativity that was piled inside my heart. My thoughts ran rampant because my heart was filled with pain, shame, and disappointments.

What if our hearts are the puppet masters to our feelings? See, the heart controls the mind. Most people believe that we think and then we feel. On the contrary, feelings come first, and then later thoughts are executed. When my son fell, he instantly cried. He did not think of the pain and then cry. His first reaction was what he *felt* which was pain. This is the reason God urges us to guard our hearts for out of it springs the issues of life. [Proverbs 4:23]

The internal conflicts I struggled with began as a child; however, the manifestation of those issues occurred in adulthood. The issues in my heart, impeded my flight to success and created imaginary limitations. Although imaginary, I felt them as real. This is how trauma affects us. Those perceived limitations turned into frustrations which boiled up like a pile of acid spewing from a battery, which is corrosive to the environment. When the acidity in my battery interacted with people, I self-sabotaged relationships unknowingly because I did not know how to handle everything I felt on the inside. There were no words that I could use to verbalize what I felt; I just reacted. I walked in offense, I lived in offense lane. My anger was loud, and it was not backing down! The only real solution for me was to find the fragmented girl in my past. The problem was that I did not know where she was lost. I could not hand over my brokenness because I did not know where the brokenness began. My anger would not allow me to see that I was shattered and in need of repair.

And tear your heart and not your garments -Joel 2: 13a.

For you to tear your heart (meaning remove the old limited one), you must first admit that there are offenses you have been holding tightly onto that must be torn from you so that the power of the almighty God can enter in. This requires a level of displacement on our behalf; a transfer of energy to obtain healing. Again, it works in direct proportion with faith. This tearing allows God to seep through the cracks and begin to use his powerful glue and bridge the gaps with higher truths about your experiences and your true nature.

Being married forced me to see my truth. If I did not face the real hidden issues in my heart, I could not make a lasting relationship with God, myself, husband, family or friends. No one could dig into my heart other than me. I was the only one who could let God into the broken places so that he could cleanse, heal, and restore me to my full potential. I could no longer allow myself to be confined and victimized by emotional and mental distress. I could no longer be an imposter and pretender of perfection.

I had to begin to understand what emotional traumas were corroding my battery so that I could reconnect to the vine, the true sources of my power and therefore, be restored to functioning at peak condition.

During this time, I learned that starting over was an opportunity to get a fresh perspective and find the fragmented pieces of myself.

POWER CHARGE PRAYER

Father, I pray that you will show me where the fragmented pieces of myself are. That I may reconcile who I am now with the person I was. That you will help heal every portrait of myself and make me whole. Your desire for my life to be whole was so great that you sent your son to die for my wholeness and to find what was lost. Jesus is the door that grants me access to you—the power supply for my battery. In order for me to operate at optimal condition, I need you to heal the broken places within me.

Father, as day broke forth and the angel rolled away the stone and shed light in the tomb shed light in the dark places and kinks in my life. Roll away the stones that imped your healing to seep through the cracks in my life.

Father, I welcome your transformative light into my life. I place my trust in you. According to Psalm 143:8, let me know the ways in which I should walk.

Thank you for allowing our reconciliation. It is in you I live and move and have my being. I am not whole without you. Please show me the areas in my life that need repair, realignment, and reconfiguration so that I can be everything you intended for me to be. In the mighty name of your set apart son, Jesus the Christ I ask all these things. Amen.

CHAPTER FIVE

REDOX REACTIONS

How you feel about yourself determines how you deal with those around you. Your emotional state dictates how fluid the flow of electrons is in your battery. This internal process is much like redox reactions that occur in batteries. Electrons (your emotions), provide the flow of current needed to power your device. The quality of that flow, however, determines how well your device functions.

The best metals are those that conduct electricity. Within this demonstration, you are—in essence—a metal conductor. If your metal makeup becomes strained by waste, it will hinder the flow of charge to your battery and will affect either how well or how impaired your device functions.

While I was in high school, my father died of Aids. He was debilitated by a stroke, but his immunocompromised body could not sustain such stress. There were times when my father's memory was not functional, and he would find himself in different places confused. Unfortunately, the disease took a toll on his mind. I was coming from church with my parents and the family of a boy I was dating, when my father decided to jump out of our moving vehicle. He then began to run down a dark street. My mother, extremely confused, stopped the car and looked at me with such distress and embarrassment. I took off my shoes and sprinted after my father barefoot. I caught up to my father and realized he was disoriented; he could not comprehend how he made it to the lower overhead side of the bridge. Some months later my father would be institutionalized for becoming a danger to himself and others. My mother and I decided to place him in a psychiatric facility for some days, so that he could get the professional help that we could not provide him. If you are wondering where the AIDs came from, I can tell you it was not from sharing a needle. Unless, I was lied to my entire life about who my father really was. Rumor had it that he struggled with his truth. I cannot ask him because he is dead; therefore, all is left to speculation. It was a hard pill to swallow, because in my eyes, my father was such an awesome man. This dynamic person that raised me was very wholesome. My father was a militant man, yet also very loving and caring. I could not grasp how he could have been so careless when he instilled in me to be otherwise. **I could not grant him the opportunity to fail, because in my eyes he was perfect.** What happens when you realize those you hold dear have imperfections you cannot repair? My biggest frustration was that I carried his secret ashamed as if it were my bag of stones to carry. I began to ask myself "was I, his daughter, not enough for him to make the right decisions or plan his life accordingly"? I thought there were sacrifices you made for your kids to ensure their safety and their future. I felt like my father had all the right words to say, but not the deeds to support those words. I was too busy trying to connect the dots instead of loving the fleeting moments we had.

    My father's best friend, a pedophile, (whose name I will not mention) revealed to me that he was gay. I could not believe him, being he was the very same person who would masturbate in front of me and then tell me that no one would ever believe me if I said anything. My father trusted him because he was his best friend, so I was guilted into silence. I also knew this was the only friend my father ever really had, and I thought it would break his heart if he knew.

I remember when I was eight years old, I mentioned to everyone that he used to look up my skirt, but no one paid attention to what I said. I realized years later that this incident silenced my voice. I observed how he became a favorite in our home, while I was classified as the child who told stories—as if my name were Pinocchio.

Years later, I was asked about this incident and I lied yet again. I could not tell the truth. I kept this secret to myself because I felt guilty! The eight-year-old me was broken from the day that no one acknowledged that I was violated. This was the girl I was looking for as an adult. I did not know where to find and heal her.

My father's best friend fell on hard times and he moved in with us. This man lived in our home and tormented me while everyday I pretended to be okay. Since then I became a liar! See, pretending was becoming part of my nature so that no one would know what was really going on in my life. During the time this man spent with my father and I he told me things about my father; secrets that no one in my family would talk about or even admit to. This filthy man continued to torture me, attempt to touch me, and say things that I, as a child, could not understand. I used to wonder what was in it for him and why he felt like I needed to know these things. Later, I realized that he wanted to have a relationship with me. He wanted me to feel a sense of security by telling me things he felt would earn my trust. Then, he would pretend to fill in the gap for my father by buying me things he thought I needed. Whenever I saw him, I cringed with disgust, but I would put on that smile, because I knew that level of embarrassment would cost my dad his only friend. There was a part of me that did not want to be disappointed either if I told him the truth and he did not believe me. He was attempting to uncover my father's secrets so that my feeble little mind would run to him for rescue. Finally, one night he came to the hallway where my room was at my grandmother's house while everyone was sleeping in their drunken stupors to masturbate and swing his privates in front of me. I found the courage to stand up for myself and threatened to tell my father. Little did he know I was made of iron! That was the last time I had to partake of his filth, or so I thought. My courage dwindled and I still told no one. I kept all this to myself. I could not even mention it to my sister, my best friend. At this point, I began to change. This was when drinking became part of my every weekend routine. Stealing my aunt's beers and pre-gaming. Hanging out with my friends and partying on the weekends made my weeks easier to bare. The pot of bitterness only boiled without possible dissipation. If you are wondering how old I was? I was grown before I was grown!

    This would be the place I had to revisit to reconcile the little girl who was broken within the twenty-nine-year-old woman who now shares this story. My brokenness did not begin with my mother kicking me out of her home for dating someone she did not approve of. It started, the day I was made into a liar.

    The person that my father portrayed to me was different from the actual struggle he faced. Over the years, I began to question when my father had the time and where I was if every waking minute, I spent it with him. I was carrying my father's baggage as my own and it only made the load heavier to bear. I could not share this type of burden with anyone else because I did not want anyone to judge me, my father, or my family.

    The summer I began high school, my father dropped me

off to my mother to salvage his relationship with his girlfriend because I was testing it. Unfortunately, his girlfriend passed, so he moved to Florida a year later. At this time, my father decided he wanted to reconcile his relationship with my mother, but he had already become sick. It seemed like a great idea, because every year, as a little girl on my birthday, I wished my parents were back together. What kid would not yearn for their home to be whole with two loving parents? In retrospect, I ask myself, "was the reconciliation for us or for him?" I think he knew that my mother would honor their vows and take good care of him during his final days. While he was away, he did not mention sickness of any kind. Maybe he was too embarrassed at himself. I also believe he must have been in denial for a long time of the disease because of the way it swept him up. As the quick progression of the disease crippled his body, all hell broke loose, quicker than I imagined, in our home.

My father's memory lapse made him a danger to himself. He had to step down as a teacher due to the effect the disease had on his mental faculties. At times, we would have to pick him up from jail for trespassing because he thought he was in his own home, but was actually in someone else's yard. The days turned into years and the pain increased. I watched my strong hero fade away the like the morning dew.

The agony I felt only worsened through the days. I realized then that I knew nothing about my father. All I could hold on to were all the memorable joys. The memory of who he was to me, perfect in all his ways. The words of encouragement that he flooded my life with. The fact that he loved me and I would not be half of who I am if it were not for him.

As his condition worsened, I could not muster up the nerve to ask him how this happened. Now that he was gone, no one could provide the answers I needed. Taking care of him, washing and clothing him were all gone. I was in the no answer lane! I could not interrogate a dead man about his life choices. No matter how hard I stepped on his grave and yelled at it no answers would come flying out of it. I could not cause those rocks to speak. I was not God or Moses. He was dead! And I was mad! Dead people have no defense and dad could not plead his case against anything my mother told me. I understood then that she would only provide biased answers due to her own pain and struggles in their relationship. The speculative questions haunted me for years; eleven years to be exact. I could not even begin to admit to myself what transpired in my life during the time my parents were together. This secret no one could know about because I was ashamed to be judged or afraid it would bring shame to my family. I remember telling my friend D in one of my drunken stupors in high school, that I thought I had an alcohol issue. I did! Drinking alcohol would numb my pain. I felt like I could laugh without restraint and I did not have to process my father living with AIDS and all the lies I had to keep up with. I would drink every weekend and she would come to my rescue. D was part of the thickened plot without really knowing how much I really appreciated someone being there. I felt a sense of responsibility for his demise; although, I was not at fault. I grew bitter over the next few years and hatred seeped deeper into my heart with each passing day. Finally, when I became a believer, I stopped drinking completely. I figured if I continued to drink the way I did, I would be dead by the age of twenty-nine or needing a liver transplant to survive. I then began to create perfect portraits and I hid behind my faith masking the real issues in my heart. **There is a difference between hiding behind your faith and living in Faith.** When you live your faith, you can be honest with people about the trials and tribulations you have faced. When you hide behind your faith, you mask those experiences with fairytale beginnings and endings. These trials shook the core foundation of my teenage life and unknowingly bled into my adulthood. My marriage suffered for it and so did my parenting. I could not walk away from my faith because at I had an encounter with the living Elohim, but I surely was mad at God. I was mad with everyone including myself. The life of my battery began to gradually diminish over the years until I was almost completely depleted. I remember during these difficult times we were looking for refuge in our church. Is this not the place where you can find like-minded refuge? We told the church we were attending at the time that my father had AIDS so that they could pray for us. I figured if we are in the faith why not find some people who would help us pray for his healing and wholeness. That was the biggest mistake we made. I can laugh about it now. The first time we were open about something so dear we were met with apprehension. Rightfully so. You tell someone that you have been infected and have AIDS and they think if you cough around them, they will contract the disease. In fact, I remember my friend and his brother who I was dating, were all driving home one night and he said "I was told by the pastor that I should be careful around you and your father because if a mosquito bites your dad and bites me then I can contract the disease." I felt my soul leap out of my body that night. It was as if a dagger were driven from my back into my heart; I could not even verbalize the sting. I knew that we were a topic of discussion. Had they used wisdom to answer their own ignorant qualms this hurtful comment would have never been made. I know that people have a misconception of how AIDS is contracted, but I could not forgive them for that. I could not give them the opportunity to fail, because they were the church. I was not taught about our humanity; I was taught perfection. Why were they not perfect? I had never before felt hate in my heart until it started brewing during this place in time. I realized I was around people who thought exceedingly small. I needed to run, but I did not. My desire for company was greater because it kept me from thinking or feeling. This religious envelope I was basking in was much better than the admittance of the pain I felt. I experienced so much during that time; everything from church hurt—to my entire life being turned upside down—to then being estranged from my mother for seven years. Talk about toxic waste! I was the perfect formulation of toxic waste. This metal conductor was losing its conductive ability. The life of my battery was at stake. I did not know how to regain control and release all the hate I felt within me—including the hate I felt towards myself. I could not forgive them, because I could not forgive myself for being involved with such ignorance.

    At times, we hide in church and think being busy is the solution to our issues and it is not. For us to live and move, we need to give God our inner most parts.

"For in him we live, and move, and have our being" -Acts 17:28

    Our entire existence is predicated upon our ability to have inward truth. This truth is what makes our metal beings active conductors for power. An imbalance of truth creates a corrosive environment for our spirit to dwell.

Behold, You desire truth in the inward parts,
And in the hidden part you will make me know wisdom.
-Psalms 51:6

    As I began my truth walk with the Lord, he gave me wisdom in the areas of my life that needed repair. It took a decade of people walking away from me and me walking away from people to realize that I was the problem. Facing your truth comes with a hefty price because it takes digging deep and facing head-on the issues that lead to corrosive build up within you. The external rewards of being liberated in your heart is one that cannot be masked. Experiencing true transformative power in your heart is much greater than any bitterness you feel. I was shackled and I needed to be free to love myself, win back my husband, and heal our relationship. When I realized that this desert was orchestrated by me, I turned to God so that he could heal the desolate streets and highways of my heart that I was not willing to travel alone. I could no longer deceive myself because deception would hinder my ability to thrive in God.

Therefore, I had to hand over the experiences from my past and finally uncover the lies that I fought to revisit.

Carrying my father's secret was slowing killing my battery, because I could not be honest with anyone. Can you blame me? The one time I was honest; I became the talk of the town. I see why my mother gets so bent out of shape to keep this shame under wraps. As much as it was my father's secret, it was my mother's secret too. I could not forgive my father for putting us through this nor could I forgive my mother for not allowing me to be sincere about his death, out of her embarrassment.

I grew tired of hearing that hate is such a strong word. As Christians, we are told hate should not even be part of our vocabulary. Well hate was all I could feel. I lived with hate and I liked it. However, what it boils down to is that hate is a root of unforgiveness. Unforgiveness is the key to barrenness in your life. The sooner you acknowledge that the easier it will be to forgive the perpetrators in your story. Unforgiveness is the formula for corrosion in your battery. It is the strongest acid that melts your metal, which completely depletes your power until you are unrecognizable.

If you ever wondered why certain things have not yet come to pass, ask yourself "Are there any lingering traces of unforgiveness in my life"? Introspection's finest work is to detect the remains that are subtlety hidden in the dark corridors of our lives.

> *"Hating people is like burning down your own house to get rid of a rat." -Harry Emerson Fosdick*

I spent years praying for the talents that God gave me to manifest themselves, but there was always a disconnect. I could not seem to access and/or utilize them. I could not be fruitful because I was stifling my fruit-bearing capacity with unforgiveness. It was frustrating because the tides were pulling me in one direction while I was orchestrating the anchors that held me bound at bay; I was wasting my life away. I knew my calling was different, but I did not even know where to begin to make the appropriate changes to become fulfilled. I was in a depressive slump for years and no matter how much I praised, danced, and shouted I could not shake it off. After a decade, I started to take inventory of the real issues that were governing my life. I was in a prison, stagnant and unable to move. I cannot even tell you how I made it to the camp of entrapment. Nothing worked for me and I knew I wanted to make my marriage blissful. I wanted my parenting and the relationships that were left in my life to last. What I could not pinpoint was where things went south. Where in the abyss was I lost? Something needed to change fast. God would not allow me to walk in the complete manifestations of His gifts until I opened the door to the guardhouse of my pain.

I could no longer resort to thinking about a quick death or jumping off a bridge. I had a husband to think of and children to raise and watch grow. The script needed to be rewritten and feebleness could no longer be part of the text. There was this internal battle within me that I did not understand. I could not bear the site of others knowing that I felt weak and it hardened me.

How could I be a devoted Christian and feel this way? As believers it is part of the journey to feel weak and tired. Otherwise there would be no reason for Jesus to say "come to me all who are weary, and I will give you rest."

Counseling is part of the curriculum at salvation university. Judgement loomed over me and I did not want to dive so deep into my past and let anyone in, because this meant I would have to relive every moment I attempted to suppress. I was really embarrassed, and I carried my parent's shame on my shoulders like a trophy worthy of honor and it was not. It was not my job to hold on to their short comings. I did not even want to let myself in. I kept asking myself the reason for my existence and I could not find one. No matter how much my husband encouraged me and loved me I was not happy. I felt like nothing could make me happy. I did not kill myself honestly to not give my mother the satisfaction of feeling like her predictions would come to pass. By now you can understand the root of my anger, bitterness, and unforgiveness towards her.

I soon realized that holding on to my anger kept my father alive in me. Me being angry with him would cover up the fact that he was truly gone and never coming back. If I resolved my anger, I would have to revisit this story and denial was easier to bare. I already felt like my entire existence was a mistake. See, my parents were married for 15 years and lived together a total of five years. That timing may be too generous. I lived a collection of six years with my mother ranging from Haiti, then to the Dominican Republic, and then Florida. I spent some summers with my mom. I lived one year with my mom in Haiti while my father gathered his affairs in the US. My father realized that I was in distress and told my mom to send me back since I was not doing well in school. This imbalance of moving across the waters created an instability in me. I wondered why my friends would get so upset that I just got lost and stopped talking to them. I later recognized that stemmed from my instability, meaning I was accustomed to not being in one place for long, so it was easier to shed skin and start over. Now, that I was married I could not shed skin and move on because I solemnly pledged my commitment.

When I moved back into the states, my father met a woman. They started dating and we moved to upstate New York. With my preteen hormones raging, my attitude would spew out of control like steam from a pressure pot. My father's girlfriend did the best she could to treat me nice and understand me, but the layers of anger never really allowed me to let her in. After all, she did not need to deal with me as I was not her daughter. Understanding me was not in the job description; I was too much to handle. My attitude truly kept me from really having a great relationship with her. As time progressed, I noticed most of my friends had both of their parents at home or lived with their mothers. I never really understood why I was being raised alone by my father. I could not understand why my parents were not together. I had different responsibilities than other young girls did at the time. For instance, after school, I had to come home and cook. I did my laundry as well as my father's. I remember my grandmother telling me that because my dad was alone, I had to step up and help him. That was like the gold star of duty that I held in great regard. Like a hall monitor in school. This is when I began to carry him as my responsibility. The danger here was not the extra responsibilities but the of lack of balance.

A lack of balance is an abomination before the Lord.
-Proverbs11:1

Forcing your children to be adults ahead of their time can create monsters that are harder to slay. Prematurely removing a vessel off of a potter's wheel does not permit the potter an opportunity to fix and mold the imperfections. Those imperfections are easier to spot rendering the vessel at times useless for the purpose for which it was designed. I am not saying I was useless, but I was not given the opportunity to be a child. I grew up and I matured, but I was still a broken child from within. My parents were supposed to be the potters, but they did not take the time to iron out the kinks, issues, or imperfections that were mounting in me. My mom was busy working trying to better our lives. On the other hand, my father was too busy filling the voids in his life and attempting to find fulfillment.

I could not grasp all the issues I felt. It seemed easy to blame it on the changes occurring in my body, which in part played a large role. However, there was a larger hole in my life. I was missing my mother during the seasons in my life that I needed her the most. When my body and mind were changing, I needed my mother. What I could not do at the time was place words to those voids, so I acted out of frustration. My father's relationship was being tested by me and his solution was to ship me to my mother. He sent ME away! The original person who stood with him in the trenches. I thought he was my best friend. Could I blame him? He deserved to be happy too! That hurt me deeply, in levels I could not begin to formulate. I felt like a wave tossed to and fro at the convince of my parents. In attempt for my father to better his relationship, he chose to send me to live with the mother I did not know. He chose someone else over me were the words I uttered to myself as we drove down from New York to Florida in an RV. I never thought that it would be the last time he and I took a long trip together. Once I was delivered like a package to my mother's doorstep, she felt like she needed to step into her motherhood role, but it was too late. I was already exposed to being an adult that her attempts to discipline me were futile. I was already running my home and partying on the weekends. She then piled all the responsibilities of her house on me. Maybe she thought this would keep me entertained and out of trouble. In her defense, there were language and cultural barriers, so she needed help. The original plan was for her to win back her family, but we did not want to be won back. At the time, I only wanted the adventures to continue with my dad alone and our family. I never foresaw a girlfriend let alone my mother! That was not part of the plan. My father had already settled with someone else and I did not know her. Living with my mom in the beginning was difficult, but I soon stepped into my role as errand girl. It seemed like that was the only beneficial role I played for both of parents. I served my position and never had one profound conversation with my mother. She would say things like "You are just like your father". How could I be just like my father if I have proven to be more reliable to her than he was? I realized my mother's frustration was with herself, but she needed a scapegoat which just so happened to be me. She is the greatest storyteller, masking her pain, and her experiences with religion and self-righteousness. Causing me pain by calling me names rather than being honest and utilizing her story to set herself and others free. My mother said to me once "God told me you were doing drugs". I laughed because I had never even tasted marijuana at the time. How could God lie on me? She was motivated to embarrass me in front of her friends and those she held dear so that they could think the worse of me, but the best of her. My mother played the victim so well no one would believe me if I told them the truth about her. I honestly believe this was retaliation for my father, but I had to endure her anger because he was not around to get his portion. Again, and again

I felt betrayed by my parents. I was a means to an end. As long, as I was a good little pet to my mother following her desires for me, I was worth being cared for. As soon as the tides turned so did her ability to care for anything that made me happy. Can I blame her? Maybe her experiences limited her opportunities, so I became her ticket for a better life. I was an asset for investment rather than a daughter who needed love and affection from a mother who was absent most of my life. The lies that she told herself; she began to believe. This is why "faking it until you make it" is so dangerous to live by!

    I was not accustomed to having such an overbearing and overprotective parent. She was dedicated to forcing her bible down my throat at all cost. On the other hand, my father was protective, but he did not micromanage. He trusted in the values he instilled in me and I would not cross them. The reason my father and I had such a great relationship was the investment of time he made and not the things he bought me. At times, we can believe that the acquisitions of "material things" fills voids in our life; that is a great deception. It is one of the biggest indicator of voids in our lives. My father took the time to get to know me. Unfortunately, my mother's definition of care was different. She believed that provision was a form of affection and a love indicator. Rather than meeting me in my place of brokenness, she attempted to fix what she did not understand. She did not have a manual for my life. If there were, she would chose not to read it. This made me angrier because I realized that she did not want to invest the time to get to know me. Maybe she did not know how to do that? She was too busy attempting to parade her Christianity and religious works. I was not encouraged to buy into that life. Her life was not an example of a person who was trying to be transformed from within but rather a pretender suppressing all of her hurt with religious works. Sometimes we get so busy that we silence the voice of sound judgment within us. After many years, I forgave her. My desire to thrive was greater than my hurt. The volatile substance of unforgiveness had to be eradicated from my life. I could no longer give her the keys to my prison.

I was drinking alcohol since I was eight years old. I was a beer thief; drunk out of my little mind and no one knew. They say idle hands is the devil's workshop. See, every weekend at my grandmother's house was a party. Moving to Florida with my mom seemed like retirement.

Somehow, in the midst of all the havoc, I grew closer to God. I needed a way to cover all the chaos in my life and maybe find a solution to all my pain. The problem I faced was that I was doing exactly what my mother did-- masking my issues with religion instead of tackling them head on. **See, religion stifles your relationship with God.** Whereas an intimate walk with God requires you to dig deep within yourself so that you can find healing in places you did not know existed. Religion births pretenders, Pharisees that lie to themselves and believe that they are serving God.

My father and I both received salvation. I thought maybe this was the key to his healing and the key to me living a normal life? Maybe we as a family could overcome this? We did not! My father died 1 year after receiving Christ into his life and four months before my high school graduation. I dealt with it like I did with everything else in my life, pretending. My boyfriend was a distraction, I was helping a friend graduate, and I attended church and school. I never once mourned my father. It took me ten years to mourn and revisit the trauma I endured. My father being gone; I spent six months unable to sleep. I read books in 24 hours so that I could keep myself from being depressed. I would literally slap myself and cry so that I could sleep but I could not.

All the distractions were gone. My boyfriend and I broke up, I gradated school and I was no longer attending the church. I had no choice, but to deal with my problems, right? No. I found something else to avoid confronting those issues. My mother noticed my distress and soon she made plans to send me away for school. This was the best thing she did for me. Once school started, I suppressed all my hurt and began to focus on becoming a doctor, as my mother wished. Every so often I would cry, but I would wipe my tears and continue pretending. Never actually letting anyone in about the problems that plagued me.

Understanding the condition of your heart is the prerequisite to digging into the layers of issues that control your existence. Barrenness can manifest its self in different forms spiritually, mentally, and physically.

Living a battery-powered life means that you need to find the layers within that inhibit the free flow of power in your life . If you are bogged down by feelings that victimize and taunt you into metal despair, the life of your battery is in danger. A dwindling charge will hinder your ability to make the adequate changes necessary to power your life; therefore, finding the proper power source is key. As you have read this far, you can see where my battery began to diminish and loose its power. Is your battery losing power?

It was a culmination of events, that layered throughout the years, halted the progression of various areas of my life. Corrosion is the accumulation of internal disappointments and traumatic experiences. The acid builds up becoming corrosive to your battery; it is a product of internal conflicts created by our pain.

When left unresolved, these experiences begin to frame our future—absorbing our battery's potential and reducing our ability to be whole for ourselves and our loved ones.

TURBO CHARGE PRAYER

Father teach me how to function at optimal condition. As you father give knowledge and skill in all learning and wisdom according to Daniel 1: 17, I ask that you endow me with your skills. That I may apply knowledge, wisdom, and learning in all areas of my life. Show me the faults and the deficiencies within my battery. I desire for my spiritual battery to be unhindered in my supply of power from you. I no longer want to be encumbered with any childhood or adulthood traumas that will hinder my ability to fulfill my purpose. Jesus said not one stone will be left upon another, that will not be thrown down (Mark 13:2). Show me the stones in my life that need to be uncovered. Any stony layers within my heart father, I now give you permission to tear them down. I acknowledge that I need you to expose the desolate areas that I am afraid to revisit. Strip me of any lies that have held me imprisoned from experiencing your freedom.

Father, I bless your name because you are my rock. According to Psalm 144: 1 you are the one who trains my hand for war and my fingers for battle. Thank you for teaching me your ways, so that my spiritual battery can effectively do its intended work, which is to power the world around me so that the world may glorify you. I ask all of these things in the name of the set apart one, our messiah, Jesus Christ. Amen.

CHAPTER SIX

CURRENT DISRUPTOR

The current in your battery determines its ability to properly power your battery. Current is an electrical charge carrier. A depleted battery can only operate as its charge allows. Likewise, your perspective is limited by the power housed within your battery. When you are almost drained in power, your capacity to engage in various functions becomes restricted.

In an attempt of finding our former selves, we forget that we have grown and catapulted into a different dimension that our old selves cannot withstand. I spent so many years trying to find the old me that I missed out on the present me. I was so lost in the in-between phase of the process, that complaining governed the moments that I should have embraced the beauty of. I could not acknowledge that I was evolving into someone who was stronger and wiser because the only thing I focused on were the wrongs in my life. Not finishing my degree, the lack of finances, and the lack of not obtaining in my timing what I desired. The perceptions and realities we create can at times, lead us into a slump of depression which further drains our battery's power. Depression loomed over me for so long that I became accustomed to trying to erase the unbearable web of deceptions I lived in. I avoided making mistakes that would cost me criticisms. I wanted acceptance to come from my mother and my father's family members since they governed my world. Moving in with my mom meant I had to abandon the life I knew with my father's family. Adding religion to the mix, I only felt further from them, so I needed something to hold onto which was their acceptance of my life choices. All which included my husband. Although, my mother had tarnished his name, I wanted to validate him before them. Her perception of who I should have married at the time did not give room for growth just establishment. According to her, My husband, at 22 years old, needed to come with a ten-year plan in hand and an already well-developed career—this was just not realistic. I wanted my family to know that I was in good hands. I did not want to be criticized by my peers; those friends I held near and dear. I had no true sense of self-awareness due to my conditioning. I was not allowed to think outside the box, because there is an unknown that I must control at all times and avoidance of the unknown was key. What an erroneous way to live and operate! Acceptance was something I believed was earned through competent behavior and the acquisition of material things. The fact that my husband did not come with the complete package was worrisome. Diving into the unknown and unchartered waters created turbulence that only awakened the deeply rooted issues I had buried. I felt like such a misfit that I finally wanted someone to say "you did well for yourself." The truth was I needed to come to grips with the fact that I may never get that! Acceptance is an internal process that emphasizes the importance of who we are in God; therefore, external acknowledgment isn't a prerequisite.

 The fact that I did not have it all together further boggled me, because in my mind we should have already arrived.

In turn, my husband became the pin cushion for my hostility; he who had never undermined my self-confidence and strength, but rather encouraged me to be the best version of myself; to let go of what I thought I wanted and to be free to explore the unknown. Yet, I could only find myself feeding my depression. **I unknowingly utilized the negative reinforcements I habitually rehearsed about myself try to get me out of the slump, that I only further retreated to withdrawal—cutting off all avenues that would allow me to be vulnerable.** I could not be open with my husband; I could not trust or love him the way he needed because I lived in an unrealistic timetable hearing my mother's words echo in the back of my mind constantly saying "I made the worst mistake of my life." Let us be real; If you struggle trusting God, you will struggle trusting a man over your life. Especially if all you hear throughout your life is that a man cannot be trusted. All I heard from my mother was cursed is the man who trust in man. When your thoughts are governed by others, it is a dangerous road to be on, particularly when it concerns marriage. Let me debunk this theory. In the institution of marriage trust was established. God would have never made the analogy that husbands should love their wives as Christ loved the church. Christ loving the church alone should tell you that there is trust ingrained in this act. Christ selflessly giving himself for the Church should automatically remove doubts behind not trusting your spouse. It was a command! Trust also deals with submission. To be submitted to your spouse, you must trust his submission to God, as Christ was in all of his ways submitted to the father. There are people who have not had the best experiences in marriage and their advice is given out of hurt. It is so important to identify these charge interceptors and to not be deceived to operate in confusion particularly in the area of marriage.

BATTERY LIFE

Husbands, love your wives, just as Christ also loved the church and gave Himself for her, that He might sanctify and cleanse her with the washing of water by the word, that He might present her to Himself a glorious church, not having spot or wrinkle or any such thing, but that she should be holy and without blemish. So husband's ought to love their own wives as their own bodies; he who loves his wife loves himself. For no one ever hated his own flesh, but nourishes and cherishes it, just as the Lord does the church. For we are members of His body, of His flesh and of His bones. "For this reason a man shall leave his father and mother and be joined to his wife, and the two shall become one flesh." This is a great mystery, but I speak concerning Christ and the church. Nevertheless let each one of you in particular so love his own wife as himself, and let the wife see that she respects her husband.
-Ephesians 5: 25-33

Most people see marriage as a glass house that is well adorned with roses. They do not see the thorns. Did you know that thorns on a rose bush develop much before the actual flower? Those prickly experiences that allows your marriage (the rose) to be beautiful. When my husband and I got married, we used to argue all the time. Sometimes in front of our friends. I know what you are thinking that was the first mistake. True! One of my girlfriends said, "You both are not examples to us of a good marriage". I will stand by this forever there is something wrong with couples that do not argue. It not realistic. If you enter into marriage with a person who is not you, you will have arguments. We need to stop placing such a negative contagion to the word "argue". People argue, but that does not erase love and respect. I will add that I have learned not to argue with my husband in public, but to discuss misunderstandings in private. I am Dominican even when I am not arguing I sound like I am arguing. It is character flaw and I am working on it. I think if our parents were not trying to be perfect and were honest, this would eliminate all these false parameters that we follow about relationships. We would enter into marriages with clear expectations of both parties. Understanding that marriage is not an institution of perfection, but rather maturity. Less divorces would also occur.

Part of our battery's power comes from feeling significant and secure which both men and women need in order to function well. These unconscious conflicts are the wars we face, but it all begins in the heart, transitions to the mind and manifest in the physical. I could not trust God, because I lost trust in my father. Now, that I was married I had no trust that my husband could give me the security I needed because one man already failed me. Trust seemed to make sense when I said, "I do". However, once I turned my trust into action, it all faded. See, everything was theory for me, nothing was practiced because my perception of reality was distorted. Although, he did everything in his power to assure me of his security. I allowed my mother's self-assured strength to overshadow my ability to decide for myself what I wanted and needed out of life and my marriage. I found myself solely relying on her motivations to survive. This endangered my marriage, because I was now allowing my mother's bad experience from her relationship to loom over mine. When our battery is depleted, what we perceive turns into a deformed reality full of constraints and lies. The world we live in has trained our mental faculties to see only this three-dimensional realm and its limitations. We are held captive to the realities that we see around us that truly shift with God's whisper.

He lifts his voice, the earth melts. -Psalms 46:6 b

It is like we have been pre-programmed to believe that this is the only active powerful realm that exist. Therefore, it is eminent that our battery's operate at optimal condition, so that we can reprogram the highways in our minds and remove those restrictions our eyes can only see. That we actually have power to bring heaven to earth if we would eliminate "perception" and "reality."

> *Where do wars and fights come from among you?*
> *Do they not come from your desires for pleasure that war in your members? -James 4:1*

The war-like desire I had for perfection and acceptance was due to a deficiency I incurred as a child. Leaving these areas unchecked paved the way for trouble as it pertained to my marriage and other relationships. Also, not having my mother or coming from a home where two parents governed my upbringing added to the confusion. There was also a lack of balance in my life which only further impaired my growth. Then, as an adult I figured acceptance came from the demonstration of having it all figured out and that would manifest into material things. For many people performance equals self-acceptance and this is how I was taught to see the world. It is a tragedy to see life from this perspective because this nullifies faith. If the qualifications for heaven were based on performance, there would be no hope for us all. That the medical degree and my stature in society would somehow counterbalance the deficiency I had from within or that these titles would somehow justify the abandonment and codependent tendencies that made me feel like I belonged was utterly deceptive. Restoration and reconciliation are what that little girl within me truly needed so that I could be free to love and to be loved. I realized that I was worth more than all of the parameters I set in order just to get a gold star of perfection from those whom I held so dear, but did not hold me with the same regard. We leave this earth without material possessions, but with the memories we have made. When we die, we die empty! The significance of death is that our batteries have been utilized to maximum capacity. Our time has ended; therefore, we have done everything possible to power the world around us. When we stand before God, we will give an account of what we did with our time and for how we did it. Had I obtained the path I desired for the sole purposes of boasting, how effective could I be to those I encountered along the way? I would still be living a lie. **I would be a detriment rather than a blessing.**

If we would only learn to be silent. Something I have struggled with for years. Yet, He utters, *"Be still, and know that I am God -Psalms 46: 10.* Stillness is an act of submission to God allowing him to filter out the thoughts and calming the raging wars within us. It removes the anxiety we feel to act outside of God's instruction. Stillness requires maturity and an act of discipline. Our inability to be still cripples our judgment. We can end up like Aaron orchestrating the construction of an idol, because God has not sent the messenger to return with instruction in the time we anticipate. **So many times, we find ourselves making decisions that sideline us longer than we expect due to our inability to be still.**

*Therefore, submit to God.
Resist the devil and he will flee from you. -James 4: 7*

There is power in travailing and then prevailing. It is a literal effort to resist. It is your capacitors firing on all cylinders, putting your faith in motion. It is resisting all thoughts not inspired by God and anchoring them on truth.

⚡ **BATTERY LIFE**

The *you* who God created *you* to be, wants to be free! But this requires removing the restraints you are pre-programmed to believe; those which have crippled and impeded your growth. It requires forsaking the instructions of old that are not in alignment with God's truth.

Finally, brethren, whatever things are true, whatever things are noble, whatever things are just, whatever things are pure, whatever things are lovely, whatever things are of good report, if there is any virtue and if there is anything praiseworthy, meditate on these things. -Philippians 4: 8

Part of meditation is the ability to be silent in God's presence as we bask in remembrance of his word. There is a stillness in meditation that requires our complete submission to God. The current for your battery is governed by God's word which requires our stillness to be empowered by it.

QUICK CHARGE PRAYER

Father in the name of your precious son Jesus remove from me any current interrupters in the form of words that have taken root inside of me. Erase Father the erroneous ways of living and thinking that have become familiar housing for my battery's dwelling. Remove the false parameters I live by that are not in alignment with your truth. Father eradicate webs of unforgiveness that have formed inside of me and manifested as hate in my heart. Incinerate connections that I have made through words that are not inspired by you from others. Completely disconnect the covenants I have entered into consciously or counseled with which would hinder my progress in you to fulfill my destiny.

Your word says "If anyone does not abide in Me, he is cast out as a branch and is withered; and they gather them and throw them into the fire, and they are burned" John 15:6 My desire is to remain in you so that I can have clarity of my assignments blueprint on the earth. Father remove the branches that will cause my soul to get out of alignment in you. Pick up the branches which are the untruthful words and the painful experiences that would hinder my ability to obtain nourishment from the vine which is you. Father you are the winnowing fork. Clear the corridors in my heart and gather the chaff with unquenchable fire that would impede my battery to operate at optimal condition (Matthew 3:12). Refine and cleanse my metal so that I can conduct electricity to power those around me. In turn the world will see my lights power and glorify you who are in heaven (Matthew 5:16). I ask this in the mighty name of your son Jesus the Christ. Amen.

CHAPTER SEVEN

EROSION

Erosion is the physical process of the distress of your battery. What external influences have you allowed to reduce the power within your battery? Do you know that some people will kill your battery's power completely. **Our brokenness can recruit people that are just as broken as we are.** The danger here lies in the inability to heal from one another. The ongoing bad counsel and bad habits in these relationships keep us stuck.

This is the art of simulation. Aaron knew who God was and where Moses had ascended to (Exodus 32). Yet, he allowed disgruntled congregants to influence his decision as a leader. They created a golden calf to pay homage to despite knowing that this was opposed to God's ways. If you allow exterior sources to seep into your battery, it will slowly erode the plates that allow the current to supply your battery with power.

Some people are a cesspool of negativity and will instantly deplete your charge. I can sympathize with Moses (Numbers 20). He had an army of complainers around him; no wonder he got so frustrated and struck the rock rather than speaking to it as requested by God. Whenever difficult circumstances arose, the Israelites murmured and blamed him for their distress in the desert, as if he too were not part of the very same journey. All he heard were his deficiencies as a leader, that they would rather be captive than be free in a desert, that they couldn't fully accept God as the source of their dependency. This is exactly who I was to my husband I was his charge interrupter. I had allowed the expectations of unreachable goals to reduce my battery's charge and in turn I would reduce my husband's power. As if he too were not in the trenches with me. I felt like he stood in the way of me obtaining my goals, and in my frustration, not understanding the root of my infectious nature, I smited his battery's life.

I could not accept my husband's guidance as a leader, because I was too consumed by my own misguided ideas. The problem with Lots wife was not just the literal act of looking back. It was that she maintained an attachment to her former life. I would soon be like Lot's wife forsaking sound judgment and looking back, because I was lost in this fairytale lie that I believed existed.

> *For where your treasure is, there your heart will be also.*
> *-Matthew 6:21*

Some attachments interfere with your ability to see the future and embrace the unknown. I was too attached to an unrealistic version of life that I was not willing to venture into unchartered waters with my friend, my husband. I guess the abyss was more comforting for me at the time.

There are those that give advice from their hurt rather than from the lessons learned. Others give you advice out of comfort, because it will stir your ego rather than stirring certain truths. This unwise counsel taints the power and diminishes the jolt of charge your battery needs.

We must be mindful of the counsel we obtain which can either promote life or deplete the power in our battery rendering us useless.

And Ahithophel said to Absalom, "Go into your father's concubines, whom he has left to keep the house; and all Israel will hear that you are abhorred by your father. -2 Samuel 16:21-22

There are people, if you allow them, who will feed your anger, they will have you committing crimes against yourself and those around you, because they thrive in negativity and confusion. Absalom in his anger and feelings of abandonment would attempt to topple his father's kingdom and sleep with his father's wives. Erosive counsel will have you act out of desperation and anger rather than out of love. If I would have listened to those voices telling me to leave my husband because he did not have it together, I would have missed out on a great man.

"But he rejected the advice the elders had given him; and consulted the young men who had grown up with him, who stood before him". -1King12:8

Solomon's son sought advice that would stir his kingly ego rather than complying to the elders' which included more humbling advice to promote his kingship. Little did he know that listening to the wrong advice would infuriate his subordinates; making them turn against him rather than embracing his rule. He would then be forced to flee and give over his rulership to another.

How many times have you listened to the wrong advice thinking you were getting it from the right source? Then acted foolishly aborting God's instruction, because your trust was misplaced. There are people who will lead you down the rabbit hole of despair and interfere with your destiny.

For so long I heeded my mother's voice in the back of my mind that reminded me of my failure. How my marriage would fail, because I married someone as unreliable as my father. My mother felt that I was somehow bewitched into abandoning my dreams for a man. What I abandoned was her control over my life, so I thought. Soon I would adopt my mother's philosophy and mindset on marriage. Although, my mother and I were estranged for seven years; her voice loomed over my relationship with my husband. I thought I had put her behind me the moment I left her house, but I still carried the fear that I had forsaken everything for the wrong person. I had given her power that did not belong to her to govern my marriage from afar. I heard her voice telling me that I would not amount to anything without her. I thought I was cursed. There could be no way that nothing in our lives worked out. The only explanation I had was that we were cursed. I could not allow my husband to love me, because there were layers of unaddressed issues of which I was not aware. I would soon place him in a similar box as my father, one of unreliability and untrustworthiness; although, he did everything to please me and make me happy. I had allowed my mother's failed marriage to take root in my heart and distress my mind. All her words had seeped into my heart and no matter what my husband did—it was never right.

Words are poisonous if they come from a polluted well. A bit of poison in your well over time contaminates your entire being. I was slowly becoming my mother—bitter—because my life was not turning out how I expected. I was belittling my husband and tearing him down. I was becoming the preaching wife rather than the confiding friend. I was an interference of power for my husband's battery life. I was a spoiled brat with a misguided perception of marriage and where my life should be.

I was taught through the negative reinforcement of harsh words and thought that would strengthen me, so I would do the same to my husband. However, this mindset would govern every decision and every word I spoke over myself, my marriage, and my future. I became a cesspool of negativity that he had to navigate through in order to remain sane.

I spent a decade replaying my mother's words, my father's death, and all the associated painful experiences I endured. I identified that these were all charge interrupters. I allowed my mother to interfere with my battery's power. Had I not released her words and rewired the highways in my mind, my battery would have died and taken my marriage along with it. The institution of marriage was a tainted idea for her; therefore, there was no advice that she could give me until her own hurt was identified and healed. Many of us walk in the shame of our past instead of allowing our past to empower us so that we can then empower others. We unknowingly allow others to place unrealistic expectations upon us and allow their judgment to loom over us like a glory cloud. Remember, words act as charge inhibitors or charge transfers to your battery.

> *For by your words you will be justified,*
> *and by your words you will be condemned. -Matthew 12: 37*

How did I get the poison out of me? I had to tackle headfirst that negative reinforcement had to be replaced with positive reinforcement. That hating and mercilessly attacking myself with despairing remorse would not provide the internal change I needed to better myself and my relationships. This would not help me jump start my healing journey to overall health. That calling myself a failure would only hinder my progress and harden the layers within me to receive encouragement and support which are necessary to power my battery. I needed to let go of the control of the unknown and surrender to trusting God's process. To let go of the anger and allow my husband to love me out of the abundance that was in his heart. I had to stop noticing the faults of not having things in my timing, and instead embrace the bountifulness that was already in my hands.

In Salvation University, we must learn to identify power sources and charge interrupters. God sends us plugs in many forms like people who constantly challenge us to look within. If we are not surrounded by the proper plugs, the life of your battery is in danger. Our relationships should never be parasitic or communalistic, but instead they should promote mutuality.

As Iron sharpens iron, so a man sharpens the countenance of his friend. -Proverbs 27:17

It is two equal substances sharpening each other; an equal yoking, so to say.

"For by wise counsel you wage your own war, and in a multitude of counselors there is safety." -Proverbs 24:6

Solomon knew that he was not an island; although, he was king. The key to his kingship was the power of guidance. Solomon understood his discipline and the requirements to remain in his office. **This is the true definition of wisdom.** I had to get outside myself and find the help I needed. I realized I was not on my own. That I had to erase the cultural barriers preprogrammed within me due to the shame and judgment of others. That the key to my freedom and the keys I needed to identify in order to open doors for my life would come from right counselors, mentors, and teachers. Someone who would give words to the pain I could not verbalize so that I could address the brokenness from within.

I had already lost many friends, some which I had to say goodbye to and others due to the defects in my battery. However, my survival and ability to thrive was contingent on finding the right counsel. The right environment that would promote health, recovery, love and direction for the sake of saving my battery's life. I needed someone I could be honest with; I needed a mentor, a counselor that would help me find the root of this desert that I had been sitting in for too long.

Over the years, my husband has taught me so much about forgiveness. I used to believe he could not understand why I couldn't forgive my father, mother, and perpetrators of my novel. I was stubborn; holding on to these feelings, because I felt justified. Like Solomon's son, I was looking for someone to agree with my pain and justify my victimized mentality. I wasted so much time thinking he was criticizing me, but he was actually making me aware of the chains that shackled my heart, mind, and feet. I was anchored on the wrong shore and unable to move freely, as God intended.

The right counsel arouses the right thoughts and emotions forcing you out of your comfort zone and approaching head-on the kinks that need ironing. I had to learn to forgive myself above all for being a nervous, anxious, overeating mess. For slumping my shoulders in defeat. For being a victim. For speaking death rather than life. I had to understand the power of being around like-minded people who desired to grow in God. Those who understood their purpose and were not relenting until their purpose was fulfilled. People who were not allowing their short comings and experiences to undermine the best of them.

Many downplay the power of words; please be aware of these types of people—they are charge inhibitors. I had to learn that my mother was one of those people—that due to their cultural upbringing and their experiences were already handicap.

But those things which proceed out of the mouth come from the heart, and they defile a man. -Matthew 15:18

In order, to preserve the life of your battery, you need pillars of Faith in your corner. Wise counsel who chastise, encourage, and promote charge to your battery. Many valuable lessons in life come in the form of trials. How you handle those trials are the basis for your reward. God will always send a voice of correction and wisdom in your times of distress. I can attest that God, in every season of my life, has sent people who have provoked a different way of thinking for me. The problem I faced was that I was not always willing to listen. These people helped me re-analyze issues that I did not think existed or mattered.

Our external experiences can create internal and external distress causing a reduction in the life of our battery. My failure to accept the fact that there was nothing I could do to change my father's death. It took a decade for me to come to terms with the reality, that my father was not my responsibility. That I needed to address this codependency issue. That there was nothing I could do to change my mother, her control antics, and her inability to know me and love me as I needed, which was different from what she believed I needed.

Erosive behavior can stem from carrying people in your life and creating baggage out of them. These are the physical manifestations of altars that we erect against ourselves by glorying our failures and glorifying those who have failed us. For so long I carried my father's secret as shame and I allowed it to tear me apart.

Was he greater than God? Was the man who violated me time and time again more important than God? I would carry this pain in my heart and not leave room for God to heal me, because "I" was keeping that trauma alive. Was my anger and failure much greater than God?

Was this pious indignation worth the lag in my battery? I had the right to be angry with these people! Why did they not earn their just reward for the way I felt and the roles they played in the movie of my life?

All these questions only drained my battery because no one could justify the anger I felt. We entangle ourselves with people that drain our power and in turn we have no light to shed on our dark places. Therefore, our prayers cease, our confessions weaken, and we begin to adopt the lies of the enemy. We become murmurers, as Israel was in the desert. If we are not careful, we too can die in our deserts.

IN CHARGE PRAYER

I take charge today of my atmosphere. I confess over myself that I am an overcomer and a beacon of light. I am a conductor able to charge the atmosphere with God's power. I will no longer imprison myself with lies that defile my character. I was made in God's image (Genesis 1:27), so I am a manifestation of God's goodness, love, grace, and mercy.

*You word says, in Psalm 23:6, that "surely goodness and mercy shall follow me All the days of my life; And I will dwell in the house of the Lord Forever." Father your grace and your mercy is my portion. **Therefore, I will be your goodness and mercy even to my enemies, the perpetrators who have intercepted and caused me hurt.** Forgiveness is my portion. I cut ties with power inhibitors and welcome power sources that charge my battery to operate at maximum capacity. I welcome your voice of wisdom through the pillars of faith that you are placing in my corner. I welcome wise counsel. My desire is to dwell in your house forever. I operate at optimal condition and nothing hinders my ability to dwell in your house—the environment that best suits my battery. I ask this in the precious name of Jesus Christ. Amen.*

CHAPTER EIGHT

INHIBITORS

Learning to identify the charge inhibitors is crucial for the survival of our battery. You must identify which charge inhibitors are operating in your life so that you can analyze where the charge disruptions are coming from.

He said to him, "I too am a prophet as you are, and an angel spoke to me by the word of the LORD, saying, 'Bring him back with you to your house, that he may eat bread and drink water.
-1 Kings 13:18

This prophet was given an instruction by God; however, he was deceived because someone else came in the name of God to provide him with instruction. In our walk, many will come to deter you from the plans that God has for you. Our job is to identify the power sources or the charge interferences that hinder the current in our battery. The issue here was that the prophet died for not following God's instruction and allowing someone else to dictate the path that God mandated. Are you willing to die due to those charge inhibitors?

⚡ **BATTERY LIFE**

One day my mom invited a fellow church friend to our home. He was someone we all trusted. Someone I trusted as a friend. As he was leaving our house, because it was getting late and my mother had yet to arrive from work; he decided to pin me down against the wall, and press his had around my neck. He would then proceed to kiss and grope me while I calmly uttered *"I will not tell anyone, just go home, you do not want to do this."* I figured since he was already aroused and acting aggressively towards me, fighting him would only infuriate him more and his muscular built would trump me in size. For weeks, I kept this to myself, I stopped going to church and stopped talking to those in my life. I went silent. My friend noticed I had not been around as much or spoken to her, so she invited me over. I decided it would be good for me to see a familiar face. Finally, as we spoke, I broke down and told her. She implored me to at least tell the pastors of the church so that it would not happen again. As I drove to the church, I could only hear my mother's words in my ear reverberating *"it is your fault."* I broke down crying. I thought maybe I was a magnet for such debacle to pursue me since the age of eight. I confided in my church pastors and they addressed the matter, but I was so embarrassed. I allowed shame to force me to walk away from them. Once my mother found out from the church, my fear was that she would ultimately blame me for what had transpired that night—exactly what she did! If prophecy were her gift, why could she not see the distress I was in?

Why hadn't God revealed to her that I would be assaulted that night. Maybe that should have been a good enough warning for me to flee.

I knew my mother would blame me, so I chose not to tell her. When she found out these were the word's she uttered to me, *"when they come and rape you"* is all I remember after that I tuned her out. She could instead have said "why did you not come to me first?" But, she went directly to blaming me because, of course, I was a magnet for violators to follow. For a long time, those words replayed in my mind over and over. I never understood why she was so rough and nasty to me. I realized that she came from the same cycle of negativity being reinforced. She felt that it was the precise parenting skills she needed to raise me. Instead of us growing closer with age, it only further pushed me away. My mother is the product of a harsh upbringing. I know that I cannot bring my children into this same cycle of dysfunction because I do not want to inhibit their ability to live, thrive, and be functional beings.

  I was furious and controlling my anger was more difficult than I could express. Pretending was the only way that I could carry this anger without anyone knowing. However, this was not helping me, it was destroying my mind and taking my soul with it. The embarrassment made me a mark for judgment, or so I believed. I also did not want to shame my family by telling a stranger of the things that had transpired in my life which would bring shame to my household.

  In the attempts to reconcile the pieces of me that were broken; I had to revisit this exact place in time where I was violated once again. I realized that the first thing I said was "I will not tell anyone." I did not say "calm down" or "just go home" but "I will not tell anyone." I was so used to keeping secrets I did not even notice that I was willing to add another one to my bag of shame.

  I had to forgive myself for willingly making excuses for other people's behaviors and carrying baggage that was not intended for me.

  Erosion is dangerous, because we allow erosive people with erosive ways of thinking to infiltrate the layers in our battery, rendering us to a halt, unable to do the work that we were designed to do. I knew then that I had to literally go back in time and imagine my self asking these perpetrators for forgiveness so that I could move on and be free of the images and the voices that haunted me.

Mama Cherry said this to me *"while others are living, you are still holding on to hurt and they are not thinking about the pain that you are in."* I highly doubt that pedophile was thinking about how my life turned out while he harassed an underage girl. My dad was dead for me to even question his life choices or the anger I felt about them. My mother was too consumed in her religion, and forgetting what she says, to even care about my feelings. Boundaries is not a word in her vocabulary, so trying to stop any unnecessary words she uses for me is like stopping an earthquake in California. The friend I trusted, the one who violated me, was too wrapped up in himself to even admit something was wrong with him for behaving the way he had towards me.

I had to address the issues in my heart and let go of the culprits in my story in order to move forward in my life, especially in my marriage.

I did not notice how much of my battery power was being drained by masking how I felt about the people who had hurt me. I was so busy avoiding meeting the past version of myself, that I allowed the fragmented pieces to cripple me in fear. It was the fear of reliving those moments that kept me from allowing God in. Indignation is a ploy that the enemy uses to keep you bound so that you can continue to live in shambles. It is a self-preservation strategy designed to keep you attached to the wound and utilizes painful tactics to pry back the scales on your scars and revert to the lies. Forgiveness begins in the heart! Do not allow outside influences to poison your well. This includes the memories of the people who have caused you unbearable pain. Letting go is the best way to be free!

The electrochemical cells, coupled with external powering connections, provide your battery the electrical charge it needs to sustain your life. Gods words are like the cells in a battery, when coupled with the proper connection, people will provide the vitality to your battery. It will empower you to tackle those areas in your life that deplete your power. It will empower you to remove outside power drainers even if they are relatives. Because we are a spirit-operated machine, we must understand that freedom is first spiritual, and the manifestations come through the spirit to the physical.

Allowing God to showcase his power in our wounds requires a level of transparency that only comes from a desire to have inward truth.

Who bewitched you? Galatians 3: 1-3

Who caused you to stumble away from your faith, trust and hope in God? Who created traps of unforgiveness, doubt and unworthiness in you? Are you included in that list?

Now, pretend you are standing in front of those people who have caused you pain and forgive them. Say " I forgive you". The best exercise I was introduced to which freed my life from the memories that kept me anchored from forward progression: Say aloud "I allowed you to entrap me in a web of unforgiveness and a perpetual cycle of regret. I am ready to move on now and become the best version of myself. I forgive you!" If that included you, forgive yourself. Say aloud "I forgive myself!"

And above all things have fervent love for one another, for "love will cover a multitude of sins." 1 Peter 4:8

I used to look at this scripture and think that love only covered sins. When I began to seek help, my mentor said remember "love covers." This unlocked a different way for me to see God, myself, and others. God would literally be a covering for me in his love. I could welcome love into my heart, because it is covering for my entire being. How many people do you know who believe, but do not walk in love? It is because this concept of love has yet to be revealed to them. It was through love that I could accept my mother again in my company, not because she is perfect, but because love covers. I would be able to honor her, because the same fruit of love that was given to me, I can now offer to her and others. Forgiveness became more about love than about storing unnecessary guilt and hate in my heart which would hinder my battery from properly functioning. That this secret place that God seeks for us to dwell in was given to me by the fruit of love. As I have delved deeper self-love is the primary tool we need in our arsenal, because this will govern every relationship we have.

Yourself worth is contingent on your ability to allow God's love to power your battery. Love will allow you to live a life of forgiveness!

FULL CHARGE PRAYER

Father thank you for crafting me in your image. For making me the literal manifestation of your love. Thank you that your love acts as a blanket and it covers me. Show me your ways, father and teach me your paths. Psalm 25:4 Your ways of forgiveness, goodness and mercy. Who will ascend to the mountain of the Lord "He who has clean hands and a pure heart, Who has not lifted up his soul to an idol, Nor sworn deceitfully"?Psalm 24:4

Father I desire purity of heart. Cleanse me with hyssop that I may be white as snow (Psalm 51:7). My desire is to ascend to your mountain and not be encumbered by the pain and the hurt I carry. Father because forgiveness is my portion; I forgive myself and I forgive others freely as you have forgiven me. I wrap and cover those who have caused me hurt in your blanket of love. I am free to be as you unhindered and fully fueled. Thank you for being my power source and my supply of strength. Amen.

CHAPTER NINE

FEAR

Had there been any doubt amongst the three Hebrew boys, God would not have showed up on their behalf. Identifying charge disruptors is crucial to the life of your battery. Understanding that those within your circle must aid in the reinforcement of those core elements operating in your battery is essential. The conversations between God and all three of them had to be one that would not be crippled by any doubt. There was an unrelenting spirit which led them all, and allowed them to live or die for God knowing that their belief would be rewarded either way.

Why would you not want to live like this? Why would you allow negative people to disrupt your power?

Negativity only breads more negativity. Wherever your thoughts are anchored determines the power you transmit to your battery. Therefore, the charge in your battery depletes faster brooding in negativity. **If your thoughts are harbored in positivity, even when your battery is draining you will have enough spiritedness to make it to the nearest plug.** At times, when our battery life is draining our recruitment process of battery drainers is higher because we believe that by fixing others, we will help fix ourselves too. I lived in this deception for so long that it became innate to induct battery drainers into my circle. This is the art of avoidance working at large, because we can then shelf the issues we need to tackle. The greatest indicator of power sources and power drainers are those you call when you are in trouble. When you are in need, who are the people that you can rely on for prayer or to come to your aid? If you cannot think of one, I urge you to change your circle.

A certain woman of the wives of the sons of the prophets cried out to Elisha, saying, "Your servant my husband is dead, and you know that your servant feared the LORD. And the creditor is coming to take my two sons to be his slaves. -2 Kings 4:1

She knew exactly who to go to. The prophet was able to make her aware of the solution that was already in her house. The gift was already in her hands. Sometimes you have to step outside of yourself to find what was in front of you all along. Those power plugs that you can connect to charge your battery so that you can be more functional and more aware of the answers around you. The fear of losing her children clouded her judgment. However, I must emphasize that although that was the case, she knew exactly where to find the answer she desperately needed.

Same goes with the Shunnamite woman. She knew exactly where to go when her son died so that he could be revived 2 Kings 4:8-17. Our connections source is vital to the very existence of our battery—anything less hinders our charge.

Who are your circles of influence? These people are your power plugs. Are they people who encourage and shed light for solutions? Are they optimist or pessimist? What books are you reading? Plugs are anything in your life that provide your battery with sustainability and increase in power.

Anxiety is fear! This is why God urges us to be anxious for nothing.

Do not be anxious about anything, but in every situation, by prayer and petition, with thanksgiving, present your requests to God. -Philippians 4:6

If you fear the height and the depth of the mountain, it will only look taller. The path to glory will seem more daunting.

Fear will have you racing people that do not have the same destination as you. Fear will force you to abort the mission and forsake wisdom, understanding and truth.

Do not allow other people's fears to be projected on you. The people that surround you will govern the charge transfer you will need to be effective.

MEGA CHARGE PRAYER

Father I ask that you surround me with people whose batteries are operating in optimal condition. People who will not relent until they leave your mark on the earth and see you transform those around them. I untie any words that I have accepted into my life from other people's projections of fear. I will not be bound by limitations that have been programed in my mind to keep me anchored in despair. I will not adopt an anxious mentality but a steadfast mentality. I will not be crippled by lies that have governed my ancestors throughout the generations. My soul will no longer cry out from desolation, but rather from a place of thanksgiving. Father, thank you for placing the proper plugs in my life that will show me the strategies I need to navigate and power my battery.

As Elisha was the one who prayed for his servant for you to open his eyes. I ask that you send my destiny helpers who will be the teachers, mentors and counselors that will help me to see what is hidden in plain sight. (1 King6:18) I will no longer race out of fear, but I will ride in trust. I am steadfast and immovable. I am always abounding in the work of the Lord, knowing that my labor is not in vain. (1 Corinthians 15:58) Therefore, my battery must not be strained by clutter so that I may fulfil your abounding work for my life. Thank you Father, that my soul is satisfied in you (Psalm 63:5). In the name of your precious son Jesus Christ I seal this prayer. Amen.

CHAPTER TEN

BATTERY BALANCING

Words are like subatomic particles that carry an electric charge to the atmosphere. Words are keys that are used to open or close portals of access. Some words are anchored in our subconscious. The remembrance of those words reconfigures our battery especially if the source of the well is poised with negativity (which will only reopen doors to our trauma). The reason my battery was out of balance was due to the unforgiveness that was wrapped around my heart. I was willingly giving the keys to the perpetrators who wronged me, access to my prison. It was as if they controlled the amount of oxygen I received to my lungs in a tight space where the walls were caving in. I mention unforgiveness so much, because it a stiff root that hides under a network of personality traits that govern our ability to function at optimal condition. It is the primary hindrance to obtaining the necessary tools you need for a balanced spiritual, mental, and physical life. The life of your battery is dependent on balance. Everything in life requires balance. You balance equations in chemistry and in mathematics —the same applies to our life. What makes us think that balance

⚡ **BATTERY LIFE**

is not necessary in our day-to-day operations? A battery operated life is controlled by cell balancing. What you are sowing into your mind and heart is the fuel for obtaining the keys you need to unlock floods of blessings that await you and keep you balanced. Walking in forgiveness allows you to see what is hidden from you in the shadows.

A battery has layers, inward parts, and a core, which all function together through proper balance. Those inward parts are covered in layers of material to aid its energizing capacity, as well as to serve as protection. Our core is composed of our experiences, morals, and the values we adopted through the conditioning from our environments. When our core is tested, we elicit reactions that question the composition of our inward parts. The product of those reactions may be negative, and our bodies natural defense mechanism is to protect us from those negative experiences. Therefore, the suppression of those experiences constricts the flow of current to our battery changing the environment of our inward parts. What is powering your battery comes directly from the core; its structure. Therefore, it is imperative to treat those core issues, because they are the basis to the walls we build in our lives and the keys we use to open or close the doors that are at our disposal. This is the intent behind having a balanced battery which will help you address the elements that are out of alignment.

As erosion and corrosion can simultaneously occur at the same time in a physical battery, the same applies to our spiritual battery. It is a result of those negative experiences that hinder our forward progression; therefore, contaminating us from the inside out as well as from those around us. As erosion materializes from external actions occurring on the surface, corrosion does the same to the internal compartments of our battery.

The performance and life cycle of your battery is contingent on cell balancing which improves the element of safety in your battery. This means that if we are fully operational, our battery is balanced to perform its intended work. If our battery is out of balance, we risk the relationships and the assignments we have been given. I have noticed that many people in life do not understand the concept of balance. There was a time in my life where I was utilizing the knowledge of scripture and I became legalistic. I was unapproachable and unrelatable. I was overcompensating to cover my fears. I pretended in order to hide the real condition of my heart. This was all due to my battery being out of balance. Our father wants us to be equilibrated beings with all of our capacitors firing in a synchronized motion.

> *And if a house be divided against itself,*
> *that house cannot stand. -Mark 3:25*

This house also encompasses our earthy vessel. Meaning, the machine (our physical body), which contains our battery housing unit, cannot be divided lest we crumble.

Therefore, your mental and physical faculties must synergistically operate in unison. The father is one, we also must be one. Recalibration is necessary at all times, because there is an enemy who is prowling waiting to attack. A decalibrated battery will hinder your ability to tap into your full potential or see solutions in plain sight. It will deplete your power, leaving you to make decisions out of desperation rather than out of wisdom. In order for us to perform the assignment that God designed for us our battery must be well balanced.

> *A double minded man is unstable in all his ways. -James 4:8*

Part of this battery balancing requires reinforcing God's words as anchors to our core belief system and redistributing that fresh power charge into our environments as works of His love. So, it is not enough to merely ingest God's word of truth, it must be accompanied by a new action that requires fresh faith in His word in order to unleash it's fullest potential.

You cannot allow your trials to drain your charge and in turn unbalance your battery. Allow instead your battery to be charged by trials, because God remains faithful in every dispensation of time. Being certain, that God has an appointed time for the manifestation of his gifts to come alive in us. Therefore, it is critical to be a balanced battery so that we do not miss partaking in God's benefits. Being well-balanced allows us to identify the areas that we mostly need help with, so that we can find the assistance we need. I was open to counseling, because my battery was not equilibrated, and I needed someone to help me navigate and give verbiage to my pain. My desire to be fully function was greater than the baggage I carried for so long.

Freedom only comes from a balanced lifestyle. Freedom is a luxury that I was willing to give my life for. Are you?

HIGH VOLTAGE PRAYER

Father I know that a false balance is an abomination before you, but a just weight is your delight. (Proverbs 11: 1) In order for me to thrive and be an effective supply of power, I need to be stabilized in my heart and mind. Show me the deficiencies in my battery that would hinder my supply of power from you. My desire is to walk under an open heaven; where I am able to pierce through the second and third heaven directly to your golden thrown. In order for me to see as Isaiah saw you, sitting on a throne high and lifted up, my battery must be completely balanced and unencumbered. (Isaiah 6: 1) Isaiah was able to be touched, forgiven, and covered by you because he identified his faults in your presence. I too choose to admit my shortcomings. That I may be able to receive your covering, forgiveness, and assignment for my life. (Isaiah 6: 7-8) I break free of all the influences that would hinder my ability to be balanced. I reject religion, legalism, traditionalism, and any self-righteousness that has manifested from unforgiveness. Touch me, oh Lord, that I may be set free; properly scaled to do the intended works you have designed for my life from the foundation of time. In the name of your right hand, your son, Jesus the Christ, I seal this prayer. Amen.

CHAPTER ELEVEN

BATTERY POSITION

For we are His workmanship, created in Christ Jesus for good works, which God prepared beforehand that we should walk in them. Ephesians 2: 11

The position of your battery matters! The power within your battery is not only for your benefit, but also for the benefit of others. Understanding that you are not here randomly placed on earth to exist and to take up space is especially important. Your battery's power can change the course of history for your family, friends, and your community.

If Daniel were not positioned to have wisdom in the interpretation of all dreams and visions, King Nebuchadnezzar would have killed him along with the wise ones of Babel. This is the power of connection at work that through Daniel even those who did not inquire of God for wisdom would live.

That they might seek mercies from the God of Heaven concerning this secret, so that Daniel and his companions might not perish with the rest of the wise men of Babylon. Daniel 2:18

Have you ever asked yourself, who buried Jesus? When it was evening, there came a rich man from Arimathea, named

Joseph, who also was a disciple of Jesus. -Matthew 28:57.

A disciple of Jesus was a rich man? I want this to sit here with you. I was in a church once that spoke about Jesus' return which erroneously taught that we should all live a sub-par lives, as disciples of Messiah. This is an imbalanced truth. If you find yourselves within an earshot of these half-truths, run for your life as I did!

A man of influence, was able to go to the governor and ask for the body of Jesus (Matthew 58). It was not one of his twelve disciples, but a person whom Jesus discipled. Here we notice that only a man of power could have given our messiah the proper burial. I cannot go into a hospital and ask for a comrades corpse to be buried as I saw fit. I would have to be well connected within the hospital's institution to obtain a person's body.

Your position in life matters! Why would God urge you to become strong in instruction if it were not important (Proverbs 4:13)? Our messiah's job on the cross was to reconcile us to God through his death. Salvation would afford us an uninterrupted charge; therefore, the doors to heaven, the opportunities, and the benefits we are afforded through Christ's death. If we make no use of our connection to the author of all creation, we are a wasted battery. A battery that will discharge due the lack of usage and for this we pay.

During creation, God placed his energy in motion to create. Potential is the composition of our genetic makeup, but creation is a choice. As our heavenly father is king, we are entitled to the power to command and create.

And if children, then heirs, heirs of God
and joint heirs with Christ. -Romans 8: 17

As children of God, we able to function at full-charge

through our salvation. We are entitled to God's power to execute in heaven, because we are legally God's responsibility as his legitimate children. We are rightfully joint heirs to the throne. Therefore, if God decrees it, so we too have the capability to decree as children of the king. Therefore, the power of words is existential to the operation of our overall battery.

Then God blessed them, and God said to them, "Be fruitful and multiply; fill the earth and subdue it; have dominion over the fish of the sea, over the birds of the air, and over every living thing that moves on the earth." Genesis 1:28

Upon creation we were given the command to thrive which is to be fruitful. To multiply which can only occur upon creating something for increase. To subdue which means that an establishment must be made in order to overtake and have dominion. The parallelism between Genesis 1:28 and Psalms 148 exemplifies the power within our battery which we have yet to tap into completely. In the bustle of life and the trials we face, we can forget the true power locked up inside of our battery. That we can create and recreate a life where our battery is used as supply for God's purpose. That we can hijack the atmosphere and bend the opportunities we are given on this earth at will. That we can call on our destiny helpers and activate them to move. The warfare we fight is not carnal; therefore, the host of heaven are also fighting on our behalf.

For the earnest expectation of the creation eagerly waits for the revealing of the sons of God. For the creation was subjected to futility, not willingly, but because of Him who subjected it in hope, because the creation itself also will be delivered from the bondage of corruption into the glorious liberty of the children of God.
-Romans 8: 20 – 21.

Creation is eagerly waiting for you to tap into your purpose so that you can be revealed as the rightful heirs to God's throne. If God only wanted your mere existence, he would have not found this scripture necessary to remind you that there is work to be done. The power of your battery is necessary to jolt your family, friends, community, and nation. You must only decide the story you want to create. It is at your disposition. You have the power of choice. Choose wisely what you do, because the purpose for your battery hangs in the balance.

The decisions you make in life lead to the fulfillment of your battery's functionality. Meaning, God created you to be fully functional and empowered by his word.

What choices are you making right now that is propelling you forward to the next dimension of grace and favor?

What habits are keeping you bound and hindering your progress?

What strategies are you using to reach the goals you have set forth for yourself?

Have you made yourself available to God as Isaiah when he said *"Here I am! Send me."* (Isaiah 6:8b) What dreams and talents have you buried? (Matthew 25:25)

I became proficient at burying my talents because I was affixed to one-dimensional thinking. I found all the excuses why I should not and why I would fail. I could never take a leap of faith, because it seemed impossible. My fear of failure and what others thought outweighed my faith to succeed. Fear is a charge inhibitor that blocks the surge of power to your battery. Fear is the literal manifestation of anxiety which will cause your faith to waiver in indecision. I was suspended in a state of motionless indecision for so long that I lived on the step of an escalator. I was uncomfortable, but I did not know how to get off because

I did not have the proper tools to disconnect from the clutches of limitations. Life was moving and everything around me was shifting, but I could not change. It was not until I redirected my heart, that I began to understand the root of my complacency and the cause of my desert. No matter how far off track you get, rest assured you can find direction avenue.

Will you stand on the right side of history and change the course for an entire generation?

Did you know that every decision you make has a chain reaction whether good or bad? If we revisit how Israel ended up in captivity, we see how one choice had the power to change the narrative of generations.

So Judah said to his brothers, *"What profit is there if we kill our brother and conceal his blood. Come and let us sell him to the Ishmaelites, and let not our hand be upon him, for he is our brother and our flesh. And his brothers listened."* (Genesis 37: 26-27)

What a conundrum? This hate had been brewing for some time because Jacob loved the son of his old age (Genesis 37: 3). Unfortunately, Joseph did not know the imminent danger he unearthed sharing his dream with his siblings. When certain people come across purpose, they will hinder your ability to progress because they do not understand how to differentiate ordinary from extraordinary. A dim light can only pave way but so much, but a bright light paves the entire journey. Some people are debilitated by the light that shines within you because it sheds light on the discrepancies found within their battery. We learn here that not everyone is allowed to know your vision or venture on your journey with you, because you do not know their full intentions. Some people only come on the journey to see how much power they can extract from you until you fail. I do not think that Joseph's siblings understood what encompassed selling their brother into slavery, that the generations after them would too be enslaved. However, Joseph was a power source that God chose to bless his family (during a time of crisis) and also for prophecy to be fulfilled. His journey was difficult and long, but worth the while because his charge would power an entire nation in need.

> *"But as for you, you meant evil against me; but God meant it for good, in order to bring it about as it is this day, so save many people alive." -Genesis 50:20*

It does not matter what hurdles you have had to overcome. Your job is to get through them, over them, or around them. Allow God to teach you divine mechanisms to overcome.

Over the years, I have had to embrace the power within this scripture. It truly is not the person, but the spirits operating behind the person that meant the evil. Understanding this has given me solace. I have been more open to forgiving the perpetrators who have hurt me in the past. The intention was for evil, but I today stand stronger in the creator.

Will you allow your scars to be visible, so that it can be a vehicle God uses to bring glory to his name? To unify people who have walked away from him. Will you allow your vulnerability to heal those hurting around you? Your gift is needed and required to change the course of this generations. Trials are meant to create strength and durability in you so that you can teach and empower others throughout the lifetime of your battery. The layers in your battery are meant to provide resistance, conductivity, and endurance to support your core elements faith, trust, and hope.

It is our ability to see through the fire that enables us to speak about flame.

SELF-WORTH

Upon creation God already defined who you were. Now, your job is to figure out where you will best utilize your battery. Self-worth is digging another well to make yourself count. There is no need to quarrel, instead allow God's charge to create relevancy for you. Your battery was intended to electrify the world with God's truth.

Then they dug another well, and they quarreled over that one also.
Genesis 26:12

Keep digging within until you find your place in this world, because there is an assignment intended for your battery.

FERVENT FLASH PRAYER

Father teach me how to function at optimal condition. As you father give knowledge and skill in all learning and wisdom according to Daniel 1: 17, I ask that you endow me with your skills. That I may apply knowledge, wisdom, and learning in all areas of my life. Show me the faults and the deficiencies within my battery. I desire for my spiritual battery to be unhindered in my supply of power from you. I no longer want to be encumbered with any childhood or adulthood traumas that will hinder my ability to fulfill my purpose. Jesus said not one stone will be left upon another, that will not be thrown down (Mark 13:2). Show me the stones in my life that need to be uncovered. Any stony layers within my heart father, I now give you permission to tear them down. I acknowledge that I need you to expose the desolate areas that I am afraid to revisit. Strip me of any lies that have held me imprisoned from experiencing your freedom.

Father, I bless your name because you are my rock. According to Psalm 144: 1, you are the one who trains my hand for war and my fingers for battle. Thank you for teaching me your ways, so that my spiritual battery can effectively do its intended work, which is to power the world around me so that the world may glorify you. I ask all of these things in the name of the set apart one, our messiah, Jesus Christ. Amen.

CHAPTER TWELVE

IMAGINATIVE POWER

If it is imaginable, then it is conceivable. Slightly cliché, but truthful. "Come let us build ourselves a city, and a tower whose top is in the heavens" (Genesis 11:4). Nimrods vision was so grand that it called God's attention.

> "And now, they are not going to be withheld from doing whatever they plan to do" -Genesis 11:6b

God himself recognized that if these plans were executed nothing would be withheld from them. What they had imagined was conccivable! Therefore, God had to execute his contingency plan and halt the plans established by man. It forced Gods hands into action!

> "Let us confuse their language" -Genesis 11:7a. "So, the Lord scattered them abroad from there over the face of all the earth and they ceased building the city." Genesis 11:8

Nimrod understood the concept of imaginative power. Although, the intention of the plans were interrupted, we should note that God's attention can be obtained to the point where we force his hands into action.

Even Satan understood the power of imagination. He deceived Eve in the Garden by infiltrating her thoughts first and then tantalizing her with the image of the forbidden fruit. Satan knew that his words would resound and cause Eve to reason with herself and end up rewriting history. Then allowed her to envision what led to their demise.

"Don't they come from your desires that battle withing you"
-James 4:1b

When Jesus was led into the wilderness to be tried, Satan transported him to a high mountain to show him all kingdoms of the world and then began to lure him with divisive words (Matthew 4:8). The power of imagination comes from your ability to see and hear what you can become. Therefore, Satan was attempting to persuade Jesus as he did with Eve in the beginning to see all the kingdoms of the world because he understood the power behind imagination. See, imaginative power was established in the beginning of time. To create something, you must imagine it first.. Throughout time we see the ability of its power—creative imagination. I say this to say that if greater things will we do (John 14:12b), who are in Christ Jesus; what is the limiting factor to your imagination? Why have you stopped dreaming?

For the kingdom of heaven is like a man traveling to a far country, who called his own servants and delivered his goods to them.
-Matthew 25: 14

Will God be able to turn to you and say "thou good and faithful servant?" If you would stop looking to the left and right at your neighbor's talents and count your own talents, you would better make use of your battery by allowing those goods to make room for you.

The steps of a good man are ordered by the Lord:
And he delights in his way. -Psalms 37:23

Whether you are a dry-cell, voltaic-battery, electric battery, storage battery, flashlight battery, solar battery you are still a battery. What do I mean? We all have assignments for our battery's to perform. If your neighbor is a solar battery and you are a voltaic-battery you have been commissioned both to work. There is no need for comparison, your steps are all ordered by God to do the intended work he alone called you to do. This is why God illustrates the parable of the talents in Matthew. It is so important to understand the take home message that we have been appointed to perform work depending on what the father has endowed you with.

If you are questioning who you are that God would be mindful of you? What is so special about you? Those were my exact sentiments.

I am fearfully and wonderfully made;
Marvelous are Your works, And that my soul knows very well.
-Psalms 139:14

God marvelously created you. Every detail about you God worked to craft wonderfully. It was his aptitude who gave you purpose. It would be a waste of God's time to create something without function. If everything in life has a purpose and you were made in his image, there would have to be a justification for your existence. God would not have had to rest on the seventh day if he did not carefully create everything in this world for your benefit. I will say it again "For your benefit"! Let us tap into God's benefits!

If you are wondering why it is taking so long to reveal your purpose, I must ask: Have you been working the evident gifts God has given you? Those things that you are naturally good at? As you work, the revelation of your purpose will unfold. I had to decide that all the talents that were evident at my disposition I would use. I have a love for chemistry, because I understand how chemistry works in nature. I love doing research. I started writing and singing all which I love to do. I stopped pondering or waiting for some prophet to tell me what to do. I took a leap of faith and watched the story unfold as I worked.

I used to be one of those people comparing my talents and what I had in my arsenal with others. I cannot sing like they can. I do not have the influence they do. I do not have the financial liquidity to fund the assignment. I do not look like they do. All of these excuses only kept me silent and stagnate. One of the enemy's delights is to keep you from tapping into your power and making you mute. As long as the goods are given from God there is a timing for all of them to manifest themselves. Stop worrying about how and get to work. As soon as I got to work lo and behold God opened the doors and he placed my destiny helpers in my path. I had to stop the corrosive behavior of comparing my journey to others and what I did not have. I anchored my thoughts on the goods that were within my battery. Focus on getting God's attention and everything else will fall to the wayside.

Far too long you have asked amiss. "Why me?" or "When will this end." Direct tenacious questions to the father "how can

I learn to use this talent that is in my hands"? If it's losing weight, plan, write it down and take action. If it is sowing a garment that no man has seen, make an appointment with yourself every day to follow the plan you have written down. But, do not allow yourself to deviate despite what others may say. I had to learn to be accountable to myself. I had to put myself first, because I knew what I wanted and what I needed to keep my battery operating optimally. I was sixty pounds overweight after having my second child. It was hard, but I had to determine that I needed to put my plan in motion other than just writing it down. I could not complain anymore because my complaints were not taking me to the next dimension.

Right now, just drop down and do ten push-ups. Say ten positive things about yourself. Do not be trapped by condemning your life to an existence filled with limited negative thoughts; the world already does that for you. When your motivation dwindles because of the circumstances around you anchor yourself in the truth of God's words. If you can remember anything positive at least remember that God sent an entire being to die for you. That he would leave the 99 to find you. (Matthew 18:12) Do not allow Christ's sacrifice to be in vain. Live in your purpose. Decide to respond to each test with optimism even if you cannot see light because Christ died for your life to come alive and to be a light as he is. As long as there is power in your battery, there is hope to execute God's plan and leave an imprint on this world that will reconcile people back to God..

Ingrained in your battery is the purpose that God has for you. Let us find it together!

God has given us goods to deliver which we will have to give an account to him for. What have you done with your goods? The treasure that God has entrusted within your battery to empower the world. If we are lights that shine bright on a nightstand, then there must be sufficient charge flowing through your battery to produce that bright light.

When we were created, God did not spare one thing. He created the world and everything in it, including us with the power of his imagination. Now that we have become legitimate children of God, can we not tap into those supernatural powers? Of course, we can! **However, we must first remove all the limitations we adapted from our cultures, associations, and environments.** It is important to understand that simulation will cause you to adopt philosophies that are contrary to God's purpose and plan for your life. The danger of plugging into circuits that will drain the life of your battery. We must disassociate ourselves from limiting thoughts and remove ourselves from people whose perception of God is so small that they see the world from a limited point of view. We must not allow our trials to skew or derail our vision. From creation, we notice that God has fulfilled what he set for himself to accomplish. If he has placed the vision in you, it will withstand the test of time, trials, and tribulations until the appointed moment for its fulfillment.

God gave you the power to create! What visions do you have that will cause God to stop and move on your behalf?

What faith do you have that causes the father to stop and feel the pull of power coming out of him from heaven. The type of power that would cause him to place a contingency plan in motion. Are you using the eyes of your mind? What side of the lenses are you seeing yourself through? A telescope, you will notice makes the images you see from the negative side of the lenses look smaller.

This was the very outlook I had on the world. My facilities were trained to see the glass half empty and not half full. I saw God through the negative lenses due to my inability to honestly believe in his power.

How can we elicit a response from God that would even halt an impending doom? Your battery would need to operate without inhibition of external or internal factors.

How did Daniel and Moses get God's attention? Daniels prayer got God's attention to move that he even dispatched an angel to let him know that his prayer was already heard before the fast began. Daniel 9

What was it about Moses that God would halt his anger from reaching Israel for their faithlessness and inability to wait? What did these servants have that would cause God to move for them the way He did? Why does it seem like you do not have God's ear?

Ask yourself, are the ions of with faith, trust, and hope flowing through your battery?

BOOSTER CHARGE PRAYER

 Father, you have established me in Christ and have anointed me in you. (2 Corinthians 1:21) Thank you for imaginative power which allows me to envision and manifest your promises from heaven in my life. I am able to use the lenses of my mind to see and charge the atmosphere with your power. I have the ability as your child and representative of the kingdom to execute decrees from heaven to earth. That the legislative operations of heaven I am able to weld at my command. That your order and power from heaven can awaken creation in my favor and whatsoever loose and bind in heaven is also established on earth. (Matthew 18:18)

 Thank you Father, for the signet ring which is you word. I am able to release and cosign executive orders from heaven that benefit my myself, my family, my community, and my nation. That I am able to walk as Abraham walked, and request your mercy as you hear me. That I am able to activate your hands to move on my behalf. Thank you Father, for my ability to communicate with you unhinderdly, that you provide me instructions in every dimension of faith. Thank you for the blood of Jesus that is a shield over our conversations and this prayer. Amen.

Thank You!

I hope the spirit of love, in which this book was written, will ignite your ability to move. That you will begin to address the issues that have held the power in your battery captive. Remember to choose yourself every time by opening up your heart to forgive. Recharge your battery during the waiting moments and enjoy the process of time. My prayer is that through this journey your mind and your heart will turn. It is in the act of turning that you will reap the benefits for which you are already entitled. The promises of God are equal throughout the generations with one goal in hand which is to bring glory to the father. May God's anointing in you break the yoke of fear, entrapment, unforgiveness, and astigmatism. That you will enjoy the luxury of freedom to create a life that will change the world around you. You were promised the land of milk and honey. It is only a grasp, a thought, a prayer, or a wait away. May your battery no longer be encumbered, but free to do its intended work to energize and produce life.

I pray that you are catapulted into another dispensation of his grace, favor, and mercy.

God bless you!

About the Author

Clariluz Graham is Founder of the Women's Energizing Network, a nonprofit organization, which provides support and accountability to underserved minority women by connecting them to a myriad of resources. She is also founder of True Type Inc., a research and development company for health and cosmetic products. On her time off, she seeks out new ways to help her fellow sisters and show them that they matter. Her heart's desire is to lessen the pitfalls for those who wish to navigate the entrepreneurial arena. Extremely grateful to have found the destiny helpers who have equipped her for success, she desires to be a gateway of blessings to others.